SEMEIA 39

ORALITY, AURALITY AND BIBLICAL NARRATIVE

Editor of this Issue
Lou H. Silberman

Published by
SCHOLARS PRESS
P.O. Box 1608
Decatur, GA 30031–1608

Printed in the United States of America
on acid-free paper

CONTENTS

CONTRIBUTORS TO THIS ISSUE

Gilbert L. Bartholomew
Lancaster Theological Seminary
P. O. Box 283
Orwigsburg, PA 17961

Thomas E. Boomershine
United Theological Seminary
1810 Harvard Blvd.
Dayton, OH 45406

Thomas J. Farrell
Regis College, Toronto School of Theology
94 Isabella Street
Toronto, Ont. M4Y IN4

Werner H. Kelber
Department of Religious Studies
Rice University
Houston, TX 77251

Walter J. Ong, S.J.
Department of English
St. Louis University
St. Louis, MO 63103

Herbert N. Schneidau
Department of English
University of Arizona
Tucson, AZ 85721

Lou H. Silberman
Department of Oriental Studies
University of Arizona
Tucson, AZ 85721

INTRODUCTION
Reflections on Orality, Aurality and Perhaps More

Lou H. Silberman
Vanderbilt/University of Arizona

"A good song, I think. The end's good—that came to me in one piece—and the rest will do. The boy will need to write it, I suppose, as well as hear it. Trusting to the pen; a disgrace, and he with his own name made. But write he will, never keep it in the place between his ears. And even then he won't get it right alone. I still do better after one hearing of something new than he can after three. I doubt he'd keep even his own songs long, if he didn't write them . . ." So muses Simonides, the sixth century (B.C.E.) rhapsode, protagonist of Mary Renault's novel *The Praise Singer,* as he contemplates the decline, for him, from the oral into the written. "Men forget how to write upon the mind . . . I thought I'd best turn to and make a book of my own, lest book-taught slovens should garble me when I'd dead" [Renault, 11].

Eight centuries later, Papias, bishop of Hierapolis, expressed the same concern: "And whenever anyone came who had been a follower of presbyters [apostles], I inquired into the words of the presbyters . . . For I did not imagine that things out of books would help me as much as the utterance of a living and abiding voice" [Eusebius, *History of the Church,* 3.39]. For these two and for a multitude of others hearing was better than seeing.

The burden of this issue of *Semeia,* purged of such negative implications, is the problem or the problems that arise when the move from orality and its complement, aurality, to literality[1] and its ultimate accomplice, silent reading, does take place. The observation post from which these problems in this instance have been viewed is Werner Kelber's *The Oral and the Written Gospel,* a work concerned with the emergence of Mark's gospel as text and the implications of that process. The results of that examination are the objects of scrutiny in the four papers that make up the first part, followed by Kelber's response to bouquets and brickbats. In the second part, Kelber reflects on the wider and further implications of the move he has described, with a comment on his conclusions from the pen of a literary critic from outside the field of biblical scholarship.

These preliminary comments are made only for the purpose of orientation. You will have, having frowned at the mouth-filling title, wanted to know what you are getting into; whilst I want you to know just enough to keep you turning pages without making that unnecessary. My own interest at this point is to go behind the spoken written[2] move to meditate on a particular bias in the cultural realm that apparently over-rode Simonides' fictional and Papias' historical discomfit.

By the time Mark's narrative gospel emerged out of an oral back-ground that was either sayings-gospel or a dialogue-gospel, neither of which is for Kelber a gospel in the sense he holds to be proper for the genre, the shift from spoken to written had long since occurred. Or rather literacy in the form of a vowelized phonetic alphabet had already made its decisive mark upon the civilization of the eastern Mediterra-nean and its heirs. Yet it had by no means effaced oral composition and transmission although it can be thought of as the widening and the other, the diminishing circle.[3] One may argue that on the ground of efficiency writing is superior to speech; a scroll or codex is easier to transport than a person and its duplicability, considerably easier. Its physical persistence, given the vicissitudes of the human body, is more considerable.[4] Other and better reasons are undoubtedly available to explain the move from one medium, the human voice, to another, the written and then the printed text.

Without in any way denying such pragmatic proposals I propose to wander briefly and cautiously into another part of the wood. Don Ihde in *Listening and Voice* suggests, as he praises sound, that there is "a latent, presupposed and dominant visualism to our understanding of experi-ence."[5] "This visualism," he continues, "may be taken as a symp-tomatology of the history of thought. The use and often metaphorical development of vision becomes a variable which can be traced through various periods and high points of intellectual history to show how thinking under the influence of this variable takes shape" [Ihde, 6].[6] It was in response to this visualist bias so embedded or sedimented in our thought that Ihde undertook a phenomenological investigation of sound. His complex disclosure of the vast but stingily recognized riches of sound and of its manifold abilities to open up our reception (in the sense "to take from another by hearing") of experience raised a multitude of questions as I found myself hearing such strange sounds as "auditory spatiality" together with the warning that "a predefinition of spatiality such that it is prejudged 'visualistically' must be suspended." In this connection I was lead back to the cultural situation mentioned earlier, that in which orality and literality (better, speaking and writing) were variously intermingled; the latter having by no means yet displaced the former. Ihde writes: ". . . affirming the phenomenological sense of the global character of primal experience, it is necessary to replace the division of the senses with the notion of *relative focus* upon a dimension of global experience such that it is noted only against the omnipresence of the globality" [Ihde, 60]. If I understand this aright, I am called upon to recognize that what we are presented with is, contrary to my earlier metaphor of widening and diminishing circles, a shifting of focus; the center, voice, became the fringe; the fringe, text, becomes the center; but both remain within the global experience.

It is this adjective "global" that is central to Ihde's phenomenological approach; for holding it in mind, one is not tempted to dethrone visualism in order to enthrone audilism.[7] Even as this is kept in mind it becomes necessary to invoke *epoché,* the phenomenological rule of exclusion, that is, "putting out of bounds" what is not intended so that which is may, in the case at hand, speak forth. It is by intention on the spoken heard that a fuller apprehension and comprehension of the spoken written move is made possible. Thus it is to Ihde's phenomenological description of the spoken heard I now turn.

"It is in the ordinary babbling traffic which we have with others where the ambiguous richness of sound is both directional *and* encompassing that there is revealed a special kind of 'shape.' This is what is called the auditory 'halo' or the *auditory aura.* The other, when speaking in sonorous speech, presents himself as 'more' than something fixed, 'more' than an outline-body, as a 'presence' who is most strongly present when standing face to face. Here it is that the auditory aura is most heightened . . ." [Ihde, 78]. "The presence of the other embodied auditorily, in the 'excess' of the aura which not only 'exceeds' the presence of the outline body, but 'fills' the space between us is yet another experience of the *invisible*. It is in the *voice* that the 'excess' is *heard,* and a full sense of the presence of things and of others is one which calls for such listening."

"The auditory aura is, of course, by no means restricted to the face-to-face speaking situation. It is present throughout the range of auditory experience, though not always so notably as in the face-to-face situation" [Ihde, 79].

What does this portend when one turns to the spoken written move? What happens when the "auditory aura" has faded? The "presence" is absent? In the cultural area of Mark's gospel where, as I have suggested, the privilege of the seen, in our case the manuscript text, had not yet— nor for a long time—asserted itself; neither "auditory aura" nor the "presence" had decamped. But they were on the way to subduction so that in our own time when the printed silent text is dominant, even the public reading of the Bible—often paralleled by leafing through held Bibles as though to make sure—while it continues to be oral-aural has ceased to be aural.

Deconstructionist critics, of course, revel in their freedom from presence. Once the text exists, the authorial presence that brought it into existence is dismissed as irrelevant. The text belongs *absolutely* to the *reader*. This is, of course, the latest (I dare not write, last) reduction but it is a reduction dependent upon the existence of a voiceless, in the meaning soundless, text. In such a situation voice, the author's, is but a metaphor. Here it is, however, that Ihde's relative focus comes into play. What if the text is vocally constructed? Can the author's voice be silenced? Can, for example, Joyce be deconstructed? If the medium is the message, what is the medium of *Ulysses*, of *Finegan's Wake?* A text as an inert outline-body absolutely at the disposal and dispersal of the reader or the text as a temporary depository-repository of the voice-as-sound that must be heard if the message is to be transmitted? Is not the cunning of Joyce's text ear-cunning?

In the June 12, 1986 issue of the *New York Review of Books* I came across an advertisement for Willard Bohn's *The Aesthetics of Visual Poetry* 1914–1928 and was reminded of my first encounter with such in an undergraduate course in German. Here it was that eye as well as ear was called for; even in some instance ear seemed all but banished. e. e. cummings' lower case "i" must in every case be seen for it cannot be heard. There is, too, an eye-cunning that feigns ear-cunning. Alfred Kazin, in his essay "In Washington,"[8] offers us such an example. "The top-heavy importance of Washington to itself used to be disguised more modestly. Yet even in the late Sixties, despite the turmoil raging around Lyndon Johnson, he made his presidency immortal. A nervous young reporter had obtained an interview but was too nervous to make good use of it. Rising in exasperation to his full six feet three and a half inches the President demanded: 'How can you ask a chicken-shit question like that to THE HEAD OF THE FREE WORLD?'" No red-letter Bible has quite managed to restore such an auditory aura to a printed text.

It is then a step in the direction of globality that is offered in this issue of *Semeia* that had its origin in a meeting of the Society of Biblical Literature's consultation "The Bible in Ancient and Modern Media" in Chicago, December 1984. But what of the other foci?

"Suddenly the wind changed and thickened; it was no longer a heavenly breeze but the reek of the heavy greasy breaths, as though in some overgrown thicket or damp luxuriant orchard below him a gasping animal, or a village, was struggling in vain to sleep. The air became dense, restless. The tepid breaths of men, animal and elves rose and mixed with a sharp odor from sour human sweat, bread freshly removed from the oven, and the laurel oil used by women to anoint their hair . . ."

". . . the red beard reappeared at the mountain's peak. His shirt was open, he was barefooted, red-faced, sweating . . ." "He dreamed that the redbeard stopped. Sweat streamed from his armpits, legs and narrow, deeply wrinkled forehead . . ." These are random fragments from the beginning of Kazantzakis' *The Last Temptation of Christ* [5, 6, 7] and they remind us that not only is there a move from spoken heard to written seen and that, as Kelber argues, such a move is an interpretation, but that touching and smelling and tasting are interpreted by text as well. How are they to be focused upon? *Tríxas kamélou, zone dermatínen, akrídas, méli ágrion* [Mark 1, 6] are not silent text, not heard words. They are touchable, smellable, tastable so that their being touched and smelt and tasted lie behind the text's interpretation. Does not the text depend upon their being touched and smelled and tasted? These senses, too, have their aura that is diminished by textualization and yet must be re-called by and from the text. Renan in the Introduction to his *Life of Jesus* wrote: "In the reading of the texts, I have been able to combine with it an important source of information,—the view of the scenes where the events occurred . . . I have traversed, in every sense of the term, the Gospel region . . . All this history, which seems at a distance to float in the clouds of an unreal world, took thus a form, a solidity, which astonished me . . . Before my eyes I had a fifth Gospel, torn but still legible . . ." [71–72] This was his shift in focus. Kelber's book and the discussion surrounding it as well as his further suggestions concerning the interpretive nature of text offer yet another "important source of information," helping us to shift our focus and widen our experience toward globality or so it is hoped.

NOTES

[1]The usual term is literacy but *Webster's New World Dictionary of the American Language, College edition* gives the same definition for both: "the state or quality of being literate." Hence, for the sake of euphony I have used this word. It would, however, be advantageous were we to give up latinity and talk and write of the move from spoken heard to written seen. I have here borrowed the mathematical sign *vinculum* to indicate that the two terms under it are to be taken together as a single term.

[2]See end of the previous note.

[3]An analog to this may be the digital pocket calculator. It has not yet effaced the multiplication table together with other arithemetical and algebraic mental activities but it too is the widening circle.

[4]After having written this, I heard a computer scientist theorize that sometime in the future it may be possible to transfer "ourselves" into the computer and leave the tenements of clay that are, as it has turned out, a less than satisfactory evolutionary choice, behind. The grim Reaper is then no more than "Goodbye, Mr. Chips."

[5]Stephen Tyler in an unpublished paper "The Vision Quest in the West, or What the Mind's Eye Sees" argues the same point on the basis of Indo-European etymology. It is a sprightly paper but James Barr in his *Biblical Words for Time* has taught me to be suspicious of this approach.

⁶An interesting confirmation of this is to be found in the title of Kelber's draft of the essay printed below: "The Dawn of Biblical Narrative: On the Interpretation of the Gospels." That title was clearly generated by the title of Hans Frei's *The Eclipse of Biblical Narrative*. Both are examples of the role of visualism in our metaphors.

⁷I have had to invent (?) this term parallel to visualism. Its absence from the vocabulary is evidence of its fringe status.

⁸*New York Review of Books*, May 29, 1986, p. 11.

WORKS CONSULTED

Eusebius, *The History of the Church*, Penguin Books, 1965

Ihde, Don, *Listening and Voice: A Phenomenology of Sound*, Athens, Ohio: Ohio University Press, 1976

Kazantzakis, Nikos, *The Last Temptation of Christ*, New York: Simon and Schuster, 1960

Renan, Ernest, *Life of Jesus*, Boston: Little, Brown and Company, 1903

Renault, Mary, *The Praise Singer*, New York: Pantheon Press, 1978

ACKNOWLEDGEMENTS

To the editors of *Cross Currents* for permission to use the essay of Thomas J. Farrell, S.J., as revised, that originally appeared in that journal.

To the University of Missouri Press for permission to use the essay by Walter J. Ong, S.J. that has appeared in *The Oral Tradition in Literature: Interpretation in Context*. Ed. John Miles Foley (Columbia, MO, 1986).

TEXT AS INTERPRETATION: MARK AND AFTER

Walter J. Ong, S.J.
St. Louis University

ABSTRACT

To interpret, as I understand the term here, is to bring out what is concealed in a given manifestation. Verbal discourse regularly calls for interpretation, for all utterance both reveals and conceals. Oral discourse, as dialogue, commonly interprets itself as it proceeds. One of the most widespread and fundamental errors encouraged by textuality is the assumption that to put an utterance in writing is to remove it from anything like this oral dialogue state and thus to "fix" it. Writing or print removes the utterance from its author. But it only interrupts the utterance as discourse, for the text is not truly a text until it is read, which is to say, until it is reintroduced into discourse—even if this is after a hundred or a thousand or more years.

Textual discourse can be interpreted orally or textually. But oral discouse can also be interpreted orally or textually. Werner Kelber's *The Oral and the Written Gospel* explains Mark as a textual interpretation of an essentially oral kerygma. Brian Stock's *The Implications of Literacy* illustrates the tremendous complications in medieval culture, as text and oral utterance played back and forth, interpreting one another, reshaping social and political life as well as theological and other intellectual life through what Stock calls textual communities, which were centered on specific texts but were both oral and textual in operation. Among the various models which could be used to represent the Church would be that of an oral-chirographic textual community, in Stock's sense.

1

To interpret, as I understand the term here, is to bring out what is concealed in a given manifestation, to make evident what in the manifestation is not evident to the milieu in which the interpreter's audience lives. Interpretation can be applied to anything that bears information: a human gesture, an eclipse, a chart, for example. To interpret verbal utterance is to bring out what the utterance does not of itself reveal to a given audience. What an utterance reveals calls for no interpretation. Interpretation deals with here-and-now non-evident, or not-so-evident matter embedded in whatever is evident. Verbal discourse regularly calls for interpretation. All utterance both reveals and conceals. The quest for utterance that reveals all and never needs interpretation is a quest for a will-o'-the-wisp.

This simple definition of interpretation sidesteps the arabesqued intricacies of hermeneutic or interpretation theory as elaborated from the time of Schleiermacher, Dilthey, and Wittgenstein on through Edmund Husserl, Martin Heidegger, Rudolph Bultmann, Hans-Georg Gadamer, Paul Ricoeur, Jürgen Habermas, and others. The definition is, I believe, simply the most fundamental, general, and accessible meaning we can give to interpretation. Of course, it does not downplay theorizing but rather points to ground well traversed by those who undertake theorizing. For this understanding of the term interpretation itself both reveals and conceals. But in such a way that you can work with it. I often state to classes of mine, "Total explicitness is impossible." From time to time a student will raise a hand and ask, "What do you mean by, 'Total explictness is impossible'?" I reply, "Your question makes my meaning about as clear as it is ever going to be." And we go on from there.

In interpreting verbal utterance, we can be called on to interpret oral performance or to interpret text. The two activities are different, but not entirely different. The world of utterance is typically one of discourse, in which one utterance gives rise to another, that to still another, and so on. Meaning is negotiated in the discursive process. Negotiation begins even before utterance begins. What I say depends on my conjectures about your state of mind before I begin to speak and about the possible range of your responses. I need conjectural feedback even to formulate my utterance. Speaking of a given matter to a child, I am likely to say something quite different from what I say in speaking about the same matter to an adult. Your actual response to what I say may or may not fit my earlier conjecture. In either event, it enables me further to clarify my thought. Your actual response makes it possible for me to find out for myself and to make clear in my counter-response what my fuller meaning was or can be. Oral discourse thus commonly interprets itself as it proceeds. It negotiates meaning out of meaning.

It is easy to believe that texts are not at all part of such ongoing interpretive negotiation. One of the most widespread and fundamental errors of the past few generations of literary critics has been the assumption, most often not clearly articulated, that to put an utterance in writing is to remove it from this state of oral discourse and thus to "fix" it. "A poem [that is a written or printed poem] should not mean / But be," Archibald MacLeish wrote in his "Ars Poetica." There it is, fixed. But there is no way to "fix" discourse, even by writing or printing it. A text does certainly separate an utterance from its author who, once he has written down his text, may as well be dead. In this sense, writing creates autonomous discourse. But removing an utterance from its author is not removing it from discourse. No utterance can exist outside discourse, outside a transactional setting. Putting an utterance into script can only interrupt discourse, string it out indefinitely in time and space. But not "fix" it.

When is a text an utterance? When does an inscribed work "say" something? In so far as a text is static, fixed, "out there," it is not utterance but a visual design. It can be made into an utterance only by a code that is existing and functioning in a living person's mind. When a person knowing the appropriate code moves through the visual structure and converts it into a temporal sequence of sound, aloud or in the imagination, directly or indirectly—that is, when someone reads the text—only then does the text become an utterance and only then does the suspended discourse continue, and with it verbalized meaning. Texts have meaning only in so far as they emerge from and are converted into the extratextual. All text is pretext.

A distinctive feature of the textual utterance as against oral utterance is that its author cannot absolutely predict or often even discover who will continue the discourse he or she has started. Anyone might pick up and read a text once it has been set down. This is one reason why many persons discontinue writing diaries—or never start. But when the reader reads the text, the discourse resumes, perhaps after hundreds or thousands of years, and perhaps with great difficulty, implemented by laborious, self-conscious interpretive work, without which the inscription may say very little.

In this way, in their need to be uttered, all texts are part of discourse—and, as recent textualist studies have made us acutely aware, of discourse that not only engages oral discourse here and there, but also, and even more, engages other texts. Texts are essentially intertextual. A novelist can write a novel only because he or she had read other novels, or something approximating novels. A scientist can write scientific books because of immersion in scientific books written by others. Even a mathematical text is part of discourse. It represents an utterance of one mathematician at a given time and place to other mathematicians, wherever they are. All science is only arrested dialogue.

But even though texts are in this way part of discourse, the utterance making the discourse is not in the physical text but only in the reader or readers (or, originally, in the writer). There is no universal, time-free and

space-free utterance or reader: every conceivable reader comes to the
text out of a specific background, knowing certain things, not knowing
other things, and so on. In this way, though not in many other ways,
readers are like the listeners in spoken discourse. There is no universal
listener. There are only individual listeners, real or fictional, but all time-
bound, to whom you have to try to shape your discourse, with more or
less success. This does not at all make human knowledge "relativistic" in
the sense of indeterminate, floating, unverifiable. Quite the contrary, it
makes human knowledge very determinate and eminently verifiable, but
historically and complexly so. Human thought is marked not by rela-
tivism but by relatedness. It ties in with everything. No thought is ever
free-floating abstraction or free-floating anything else. To interpret anything fully, you would have to know everything.

All this is, or should be, utterly commonplace in reader-oriented
criticism and related criticism. But it is well to advert to it here because
of the need to attend to what is alike and what is different when we
contrast interpretation of oral work and interpretation of written work.

2

With these preliminaries behind us, I should like to turn directly to
the central question of this paper, namely, the interpretive interaction of
text and oral expression, and particularly to the effect of text as interpreting oral discourse antecedent to it. A recent book bears directly on this
question with reference to material of the most urgent significance to
millions of people today as well as to many more millions in the past and
in the future. The book is *The Oral and the Written Gospel: The Hermeneutics of Speaking and Writing in the Synoptic Tradition, Mark,
Paul, and Q*, by Werner H. Kelber. As no other work thus far has done,
Professor Kelber's book brings to bear on biblical study all of the now vast
and vigorously growing work on orality-literacy contrasts in a wide variety of fields: studies in oral tradition and performance, in linguistics,
folklore, literary history and criticism, anthropology, sociology, intellectual history, cultural history, and much more. Armed with the new
knowledge and sensitivities regarding orality-literacy contrasts and ex-
haustively familiar with earlier scholarship, Kelber undertakes to reconstruct what the kerygma, the preaching or proclamation of the Good
News by Jesus was like in the oral milieu in which Jesus operated, then
what it was like in the early Christian communities which preserved and
circulated it after Jesus' death before any of the Gospels were put
together, and, finally, what it was that Mark did with all this material
when he undertook to compose his Gospel and how Mark's attitude
toward textuality differs from Paul's.

In the wake of Kelber's work and within our present perspectives, we can say that, essentially, what Mark had to do was to interpret. The situation had become such that the old oral kerygma, which began with Jesus and was continued by Jesus' disciples, could no longer function effectively as it earlier had. Something had to be done to get the implications clear. The matter had to be reorganized. When Mark undertook to put the old oral heritage of stories and preaching about Jesus into writing, this was in effect what he undertook to do: to reorganize the oral kerygma so as to bring out its current relevancy. That is, he undertook to interpret the oral kerygma. His written Gospel was essentially interpretation. Early scholars, as Kelber carefully details, had some sense of the state of affairs here, before and after the written Gospel, but in the absence of today's fuller understanding of oral noetic processes they had not been able to describe adequately the oral base that Mark had to work from or the precise problems of interpretation in moving from such a base into textuality.

Mark's work of interpretation was of maximum urgency and significance because for those who regarded the original oral kerygma by and about Jesus of Nazareth as true, Jesus was the way to fullness of life and to union with God for eternity. Any reconstitution of the kerygma, of Jesus' message, in writing—Jesus himself had left nothing in writing—would have to be one with the original oral preaching in the most profound way, or for the faithful all was lost. Mark's was not simply an aesthetic exercise. For the integrity of their faith, million and billions of Christians who followed Jesus after New Testament times would be dependent upon the integrity of Mark's and others' written reconstruction of an oral tradition. The faithful could hold and have held into the present that God inspired the sacred text of the Bible, but what this means still calls for explanation when one becomes aware that what had been the kerygma for Christians before Mark's Gospel could not possibly have been simply the later, inspired textual kerygma, word-for-word.

Mark's Gospel, as the original major, extended interpretation of the oral kerygma that we have, would itself of course demand further interpretation. With such further interpretation, now bearing on the written Gospel as a text, the hermeneutic process entered into a new stage. The text was something temporally stabilized, context-free in the sense indicated above. It could be dealt with through the use of other texts as well as orally. But interpretation after the composition of the Markan text and the other New Testament texts that themselves also constitute interpretations of the original oral kerygma were all secondary to Mark's primary interpretive achievement, the first reconstruction of the oral kerygma in a new, written presentation, in words that floated context-free, visually fixed on a surface, retrievable now by anyone anywhere, as the utterances of the oral kerygma had never been.

3

Kelber's thesis is complex and its arguments are carefully drawn. Scholars should be discussing it, pro and con, and further explicating it for years. Some of its general lines of development that are relevant here proceed as follows.

Earlier textual scholars had understandably thought of the oral kerygma, even when they were quite explicit about its orality, more or less in accordance with textual models: sayings were the sort of thing you found in texts, only they had not been written down. In this framework, scholars have looked, rather helplessly, for the "original" oral utterances, as one might look for an original or first text (Kelber, 1983:xv). Oral utterances do not have originals quite as texts do. Texts provide what has been called autonomous discourse, context-free. Although textual utterance grows out of social settings and may refer to social settings, the text as text carries with it no real social setting such as always envelopes oral utterance. Texts consist only of words inscribed on a surface. Written words can derive directly from other written words, as when a scribe makes a faithful copy of a text. But oral utterances cannot derive simply from other oral words.

Each oral utterance emerges from a situation that is more than verbal: a certain person or persons at this time situated in living relationship with a certain other person or persons. The repetition of oral utterance is itself not context-free. Certain persons may find themselves in a given situation that brings to mind a wise observation generated in an earlier, somewhat similar situation. The observation is repeated, most often not verbatim, but, even if verbatim, with a slightly different bearing, for its meaning includes its interaction with and adjustment to the real situation that now elicits it. The quest for an "original" utterance in this real, oral setting is quixotic, for each utterance emerges not simply from an earlier utterance but from a new new existential context. In oral cultures, even a fixed, formulaic saying is thus continuous with life more than it is continuous simply with other formulaic sayings.

Jesus' own words were subject to the rules of oral commerce: they were never context-free. The meaning of each oral utterance had to be gathered from the extraverbal as well as the verbal components. There was no way for Jesus to provide to the hundreds of different people he addressed orally in countless different situations a line of discourse such as one can find in an extended text. Doing so would have distorted his message or even have falsified it, and very likely have made it boring instead of dynamic, as it was. One has to discard the hermeneutic notion of "a tightly knit community of early Christians committed to the preservation and transmission of a single Gospel" (Kelber, 1983:31), that is, of a single set of fixed sayings of and about Jesus. Both Jesus' oral sayings and the oral memory of them were always contextual, though they of course could have widespread relevance. He spoke in every case in a context of real concerns of real people in real social structures. Jesus' disciples, introducing his oral sayings orally into various contexts, lived in the same noetic economy, dipping into the store of his sayings and deeds for what was apropos in a given kerygmatic setting, for what would clarify and be clarified by a given state of affairs.

Giving some linearity to the mosaic configuration of such an oral kerygma meant decontextualizing the oral sayings by means of writing— of course only to a degree, since the Gospel text often states the setting of a given saying, but to a highly significant degree because a verbally stated setting itself is necessarily of a different order of existence from a real setting. A real setting is dense, never fully verbalized or verbalizable, involving all sorts of elusive but real imponderables. The real setting contours the saying designed for it, or elicited by it. Oral teaching must be "perceived as a speaking of living words in social contexts" (1983:33), and one must discard Rudolph Bultmann's model of an automatic evolutionary progression toward textual linearity which Mark's Gospel simply culminated as well as Birger Gerhardson's model of passive transmission of a set of decontextualized oral sayings which people memorized verbatim and passed on (1983:1–43). Mark's Gospel does not simply culminate orality but also runs counter to orality in being a "writing project" (1983:91). This Gospel "is an act of daring and rife with consequences. . . . The voiceprints of once-spoken words have been muted. This is an extraordinary undertaking. . . . For the moment, language has fallen silent: the ground of Jesus' speech and that of his earliest followers is abandoned. . . . The text, while asserting itself out of dominant oral traditions and activities, has brought about a freezing of oral life into textual still life. . . . Mark's writing manifests a transmutation more than mere transmission, which results in a veritable upheaval of hermeneutical, cognitive realities. . . ."

What Mark undertook to do was to produce something that could never have existed as such before, though its elements existed. He undertook to produce and did produce a unified narrative, with some items thoughtfully and programmatically subordinated to others, with a focus or point of view shaped not by a particular audience such as a preacher or speaker was always faced with, but a point of view shaped by his sense of the way the kerygma had to be organized to make it most effective for Christians generally who had been through the sacking of Jerusalem and the destruction of the Temple. Mark's organization was not so tight as a writer might produce today, but it clearly had a beginning, a middle, and an end. It opens, "Here begins the gospel of Jesus Christ, the Son of God" (Mark 1:1). Could any oral presentation of Jesus' teachings have begun, or even been conceived of, that way and carried through with the linearity that such a beginning presages? In Mark's chirographic organization of the kerygma, certain leading ideas develop, notably the well-known Markan idea of the Messianic secret: Jesus has a deeper meaning and message that the disciples at first had not at all fully understood and that all Christians must now understand if their faith is to survive. Mark's text, his gospel as a whole, was to present this deeper signification, centered ultimately in Jesus' person.

Of course, Mark's textuality, real though it is, never obliterates his oral sources. Not only do these provide his material, but also his writing style is residually oral. Discussing "heroic stories," "polarization stories," "didactic stories," and "parabolic stories" about Jesus in Mark, Kelber shows how these genres provided ways of digesting Jesus' work which were accommodated to oral noetic structures and oral memory. Underneath Mark's "intricate tapestry of linguistic patterns" in his Chapters 1–13, there lies a "storied, oral heritage" where formulaic links, pleonasm, iteration, the paratactic *kai* ("and"), produce a narrative that lines up episodes "like beads on a string" (1983:65) and thereby creates a sense of spontaneity. Mark's textual world remains in many ways an orally styled textual world, where deeds and words are interchangeable (the exorcism in 1:27 is interpreted as though it itself "said" something, the exorcism itself is said to be "a new teaching! With authority. . . .").

In oral cultures words are more or less continuous with the rest of life, not so much part of a separate world as they appear to be in texts. "Mark shares the oral conviction that truth is not to be known nor redemption to be had by concepts estranged from life" (1983:70). In the oral world on which Mark's Gospel draws, "if Jesus is to be continued in the hearts and minds of people, then he must be filtered through the oral medium. What is summoned for transmission is fashioned for mnemonic purposes and selected for immediate relevance, not primarily for historical reasons" (1983:71). It has often been pointed out by Albert B. Lord and others that oral cultures do not generate even approximately complete biographies of their heroes or historically complete accounts of events. Or, to put it another way, oral transmission does not present anything like an academic "course" in "the life of Jesus," "the thought of Jesus," or "the theology of Jesus' parables". It favors individual, episodic stories about or sayings of Jesus, each of which can have an immediate, existential relevancy. In an oral world, narrative and other discourse must always be tailored to here-and-now communal expectations (it may of course attack these, but to do so it must touch them), just as social realities must in turn be validated, given meaning, in linguistic terms. The result is what Jack Goody and Ian Watt style the homeostatic balance of oral cultures, a continuous process of adjustment whereby linguistic expression and social actuality interact with and adjust to one another (1983:92).

Writing disrupts this homeostatic balance, for it "accords language a separate, bodily entity" in which "meaning may be suspended and hermeneutical ratification delayed." The author of a text "loses control over the process of interpretation." Yet text needs interpretation commonly far more than oral discourse, which tends to interpret itself in living exchange between speaker and hearer, as earlier noted. Thus Mark's conversion of the oral kerygma into a text disrupts the original living, oral synthesis. Oral or residually oral people are well aware of the problem here, and Lukas Vischer has pointed the anxiety of early church Fathers regarding the way in which their own writing might compromise the living Christian gospel (Kelber, 1983:92–93). Katherine O'Brien O'Keefe (1983) has documented more recently similar misgivings in Aldhelm and other Old English writers about the newly introduced technology of writing, which they—as the early church Fathers before them—nevertheless used and developed, despite their uneasiness.

There are marginal situations between orality and textuality of course. In treating the world of oral commerce, Kelber does not preclude the disciples' use of notes and other textual aids to some degree, but he shows how, in the absence of any continuous text, the use of such aids was necessarily subject to "an oral ontology of language" (1983:91). To this one might add that the use of notes was always exceedingly cumbersome by modern standards in a culture where paper was unknown: wax-surfaced wooden tablets and stiff, bulky parchments are not so manageable as paper notebooks and, indeed, are not even very readily portable. The quite commonly postulated Q *(Quelle)* document, antecedent to Mark, would appear to lie on the margin between orality and full textuality. Q was apparently an agglomeration of disjunct sayings and incidents rather than an organized narrative.

In the transit from orality to textuality, Paul appears as a counterfoil to Mark in Kelber's account. "Faith comes through hearing" (Rom. 10:17). "The letter kills, the spirit gives life" (2 Cor. 3:6). Paul's hermeneutic is basically oral, though not entirely so, for he does appeal to written authority, as in 1 Cor. 1:19 and 3:19—"Scripture says . . ." And he himself of course writes—but letters rather than a Gospel. Kelber notes that whereas the narrator Mark retreats behind his narrative text so as virtually to disappear, Paul himself very much emerges in the text of his letters, which are thus more closely linked with orality than written narrative is. Paul's favoring of the oral charism shows up also in what Kelber styles his "deep-seated anxiety" over the written Torah or Law (1983:151–164).

Carefully nuanced to allow for convergent and divergent currents and countercurrents, Kelber's meticulous study shows, in sum, that the movement from the oral kerygma to the written Gospel is not simply a linear movement but in significant ways an antithetical one, involving a transformation of thought forms and of consciousness itself. Our recently acquired knowledge of the psycho-dynamics of oral noetic and cultural processes has brought out the antithetical relationship of textuality and orality in ways never before possible.

One of Mark's major themes, the one advertising the discontinuity of oral sayings and text, is the failure of the disciples to comprehend the full meaning of Jesus' sayings and of his life and death. The simple oral proclamation of Jesus' presence would no longer suffice. In the light of the disasters that had beset Christians by Mark's time—war and persecution, the sack of Jerusalem and dispersion of its inhabitants (Mark 13:3–20)—the simply oral proclamation of Jesus' presence among human beings no longer was effective enough. Crises generated unreal presences. In times of such disasters, oral proclamations of false Messiahs abound: "If anyone tells you, 'Look, the Messiah is here!' 'Look, he is there!' —do not believe it. False messiahs and false prophets will appear performing signs and wonders to mislead, if it were possible, even the chosen" (Mark 13:21–22). What was needed was not simple proximity to someone present, which orality gave, embedding each utterance in the here-and-now, but also distance—the distance for reflection which textual organization can provide, Derrida's *différance*—and which makes for a truly historical understanding. The kingdom Jesus preached has "a history mysterious in its entirety." Oral sayings are "too discrete, direct, and episodic to allow full revelation of the kingdom's mysterious history" (1983:101). Oral noetic processes bind the kerygma too much to the immediate social actuality for it to have its full effectiveness after a certain time. At this point, writing is necessary to present the fuller story of Jesus in some directional form, and the story cannot be a mere concatenation of earlier sayings by and about Jesus. It has to be recast for readers most of whom Mark could never hope to know. Once we understand the situation here, it is evident that the historical Jesus has to be discovered not by simply studying the text but by seeing the complex relationship of the Gospel text to the earlier oral noetic world in which Jesus lived. The relationship of this oral world to text is not one-to-one, although it is very real and not irrecoverable if we allow for its complexities. For what Mark wanted clearly to present was the real Jesus of Nazareth. Only now, textually.

4

The magnitude of Mark's task should not be underestimated. The textualization of the Christian kerygma was a special event in the history of textualization because the oral kerygma itself was so centered in the person of Jesus and in personal, loving identification with him. The focus on the person of Jesus comes clear in every book of the New Testament, including Pauline letters antecedent to Mark's gospel. It is unquestionable that Jesus was the personal center of the oral kerygma from the start. The relationship of the sacred texts of the world's larger religions to the founders of these religions differs in each case. For example, Buddhist texts postdate the life of the Buddha (Siddartha Gautama, c. 563–c. 483 B.C.) by centuries and variant canons define individual Buddhist sects, whereas the Koran is coeval with Muhammad himself: John Burton's recent work (1977) has undertaken to show that the text is actually Muhammad's own.

In Mark's presentation, Jesus' mission is the preaching or proclamation of the Good News: "that I may proclaim the good news. . . . That is what I have come to do" (Mark 1:1; cf. Mark 1:14–15, 38–39). This heralding of the Good News was an activity which Jesus had his disciples also take up (3:14, 6:12). The disciples learned by attending on Jesus and listening to him, not by reading, and are trained to be activists, preachers, interacters with people, not readers. Their obligation is remembering (Kelber, 1983:96), not memorization, which is not the same as remembering (Ong, 1967:23, 168–169). Ultimately Jesus makes the kerygma, that is, the personally interactive proclamation of the Good News, the mission of the entire Church (13:10, 14:9).

The Good News that Jesus proclaims is fundamentally the mystery of the kingdom (Mark 4:11), at the heart of which is Jesus' own identity as a person sealed by his passion and death (8:32). Jesus preaches complete personal attachment to himself on the part of his disciples (8:20–25), leading to the sharing of his passion and death (8:34–35, 10:35–40). Jesus is the Son of God (1:1) and the kerygma he preaches is the way to the Father (13:32–37), whom Jesus calls on in his passion (14:36) and who is the disciples' Father also (11:25). The kerygma or proclamation which the written text works up out of oral tradition is thus not simply a series of more or less unified exhortations or observations about a state of affairs, human and/or divine, but is intimately involved with and hinges on the personal identity of Jesus, of his followers, and of the Father himself. The kerygma, the Good News, is not simply about Jesus. It is Jesus. "Your faith in me shall be shaken. . . . But after I am raised up, I will go to Galilee ahead of you" (14:27–28). And it involved not merely the thoughts and actions but the entire persons of those he came into contact with, directly or through his disciples. The kerygma was both public and intensely personal.

The textualization of such a message, taken from an oral, person-to-person context, is a formidable one, for the relationship of person to person in a text is essentially indirect, and particularly in a narrative (by comparison with an epistolary text). Not long after Mark, the Gospel according to John would proclaim Jesus as the Word of God—certainly not by analogy with the written word of human beings but with the spoken word, which thus in the last of the four gospels asserts its ascendancy over the written text. "In the beginning was the Word; the Word was in God's presence, and the Word was God" (John 1:1).

5

It would be tempting to reduce the antithesis of textuality and orality to simple destructiveness. But the relationship of writing and orality is far more complex than such reductionism would allow. Putting a strain on a system does not necessarily mean destroying it: the strain might even improve the system, or force it to improve itself. For there are no totally closed systems.

The subversion of orality by writing was gradual, and of course has never been complete. Between biblical times and our own, orality throve in various degree of integrity or disarray and interacted vigorously with textuality to a degree that literates have tended to forget. As Kelber takes pains to point out (1983:93), "it is not within the power of a text to stem the flow of spoken words." Mark's text did not at first change the oral climate much at all. Kelber calls attention to Helmut Koester's findings that the writings of the Apostolic Fathers (A.D. 95–150) rarely cite the sayings of Jesus verbatim from Markan or other texts. Their citations are not usually textual derivatives at all but normally variant continuations of the old oral transmission. Only at the time of Justin Martyr, in the mid-second century, did verbatim citations from the synoptic gospels, most notably Matthew and Luke, begin to supersede oral transmission. From this point on, the oral way of life was more seriously contested, for "speaking was no longer the dominant, life-giving force in Christianity" (1983:93–94) that it earlier had been.

Yet orality remained a powerful force in culture. First, as we need constantly to remind ourselves, until the past three centuries or so, few Christians—and, indeed, few human beings of any religious affiliation or of none—have been able to read and write. Those who wrote left verbal records behind them, and we tend to take the mentality these records represent as typical of the entire culture, though it could hardly have been so. Studies of orality have lately awakened us to the limitations of earlier historiography which looked to the "high" culture of literates or of classes operating in close touch with literates—such as the noble or landed or military classes of Europe—as representative of most things in the culture worth attending to. Such literary exclusionism, however unwittingly practiced, can vitiate textual hermeneutic itself, giving rise to the futile quest for a historical Jesus to be reconstructed directly from the biblical text without allowance for the tensions between the text and the quite different, nontextual, oral psychodynamics of the world in which Jesus lived and thought and preached and did good works.

Second, we need to be aware how residual orality can envelop even a highly developed textuality (Ong, 1958). For example, as Hajnal has shown (1954:64), in and around the universities of the Middle Ages, despite the fact that universities were far more committed to literacy than antiquity had ever been, the vast amount of writing generated by the universities was actually at the service of orality—though, of course, an orality whose thought processes had been infiltrated by literacy to a degree. In medieval universities no one was ever tested academically by having to write anything. All assaying of intellectual prowess and accomplishment was oral, in disputations and the like, so that the intellectual world, while styled largely by writing, was in performance oral to a degree difficult for high-technology literates to conceive.

6

What was the hermeutic situation in cultures which mingled an intensive textuality with a high residual orality, such as those of the European Middle Ages? Only recently have in-depth studies of such questions begun to appear. Let me here attend to one, the recent book by Brian Stock, *The Implications of Literacy: Written Language and Models of Interpretation in the Eleventh and Twelfth Centuries.*

Although medieval culture was marked by bewildering orality-literacy relationships, among literates literacy was ideologically triumphant. The "most injurious consequence of medieval literacy," Stock finds (1983:31), was "the notion that literacy is identical with rationality." This of course meant Latin literacy, since the vernaculars, even the very few that were written at all, were not yet developed to handle highly abstract, analytic thought. Diglossia, with a "high" language chirographically managed and a "low" or vernacular language orally managed, created a special hermeneutic climate. Because the "high" language, Latin, had become a foreign tongue for all its users, the native, oral tongue of no one any longer, unknown to anyone who could not write it, it evoked a textual world even when it was spoken, as it was by millions of persons (almost without exception males) over the centuries. Under such circumstances, culture was centered, so far as literates were concerned, not simply on literacy—the ability to read and write a basically spoken tongue—but upon textuality, upon extant texts as objects in which all language and thought worth attending to ultimately lodged.

Such textuality had widespread implications and effects. For example, liturgical worship, which is normally and necessarily connected with extraliterate life, declined and theological scholarship grew vigorous. The priest-king, integrated into an "oral, pictorial, gestural, and liturgical culture," gave way to the desacralized law-king, linked to "the literate, the administrative, the instrumentally rational, and the constitutional"

(1983:33). Whereas at the beginning of the eleventh century illiteracy was
no disability for administrators, who could hire scribes to handle what
little documentation there was, two centuries later illiteracy was disab-
ling for administrators, though not in the same way everywhere. Stock
details scores of other widely diversified effects of the growth in literacy,
though the range of literacy was always severely limited by modern high-
technology-society standards.

Stock makes clear, however, that writing did not simply take over the
culture but created all sorts of complicated interdependencies between
itself and the underlying oralities. Some of the most complex developed
in the "textual communities" to which Stock devotes a great deal of his
book and which are relevant to our concerns here with biblical text and
interpretation. Textual communities are "groups of people," not necessarily all literate, "whose social activities are centered around texts, or
more precisely around a literate interpreter of them" (p. 522). Such
communities are pivotal in the development of a vast array of interpretive
phenomena: for example, in the organization of reform groups attacking
nepotism, nicolaitism, and other widespread objectionable practices, in
disputes about the eucharist that virtually created eucharistic theology,
in the making and unmaking of heresies, in the revision of philosophical
and theological concepts of "nature," in the rise of intellectualism, and in
much else. Stock's perspectives reveal the universities, which began in
the Middle Ages, as not unlike the textual communities he treats of. The
universities were organized around a body of texts subjected to programmatic interpretation which could diversify and divide the university
textual community into subcommunities or schools of interpretation. The
paideia of Greek and Roman antiquity did not function by textual interpretation the way universities did—and to an extent still do. But textuality, to the modern mind the protosymbol of order, could in fact be
highly disruptive, Stock points out (1983:9 and *passim*), in orally organized society: it undid longstanding and effective oral institutions to
impose its own new organization.

The textual communities which Stock studies generated not only
many texts but also, and perhaps even more, vigorously charismatic oral
performance, such as that of the illiterate French peasant Leutard
(pp. 101–106). Orality and literacy contrasts often polarized issues. The
popular oral account of Leutard describes the rapport between Leutard
and his audience behaviorly (orality tends normally to coalesce words and
deeds), whereas the analysis worked up by literates interprets Leutard's
activity in terms of isolated, definable doctrines (1983: 103–103). But
polarization could also be convoluted. The Pataria reform movement in
Milan raised its following largely through oral preaching (p. 166), though
at its core it was a confederation of literates. Yet, despite its literate core,
it found itself fiercely attacked by the highly literate Arnulf of Milan, who

attributed its success with the oral populace to the election of a country-born archbishop who was illiterate (*idiota,* an "idiot," a common term for one unskilled in Latin literacy). The milieus Stock studies preserve conspicuously, in their writing as well as in their oral performance, the agonistic lifestyle that is one of the hallmarks of primary oral cultures (Ong, 1967, 1981, 1982), and that still marks the still highly oral Mediterranean region (Peristiany, 1966), on which Stock's attention concentrates.

Stock's work shows the interplay between oral and charismatic interpretation of texts and the more analytic textual interpretation of texts. All the texts back of Stock's interpretive communities were not biblical, but most of them appear to have been and those that were not, including texts that were only putative (as Stock notes some were—p. 105), were interpreted after the manner followed for biblical texts. That is, the textual communities organized themselves around interpretations of texts as impinging on the world of human action, particularly in its moral aspects. Thus texts did not stand on their own but were taken as meaningful in the context of nontextual life, including nonverbal life—that is, as involved in the total social setting. A text could be objectionable not only because of what it said but also because of the one who wrote it. Interpretation of verbalization in terms of total setting is characteristic of oral cultures. The written text was to this extent still being processed or interpreted orally.

7

The notion of a textual community is far from being entirely new. It is related to, but not quite the same as the "interpretive communities" that Stanley Fish (1980) and others write about. Interpretive communities are less tightly organized around specific texts, but are rather held together by a hermeneutic heritage applicable to any number of texts or any text. Textual communities are held together by a specific text or texts subject to competing interpretations from outside. Today's vast literature on intertextuality and on interpretive communities has made it quite clear that texts come into being through interaction with other texts and are interpreted in traditions worked out by specific groups engaged with other texts. But intertextual analysis has commonly paid relatively little attention to the interaction between texts and their circumambient orality. The orality of a milieu can deeply affect both the composition of texts and their interpretation. Orality-literacy contrasts and interactions, we must remind ourselves, involve not merely different "channels" for units of "information" but different noetic worlds and different psychodynamics.

In the history of textual study the Bible occupies a unique place. The greatest unitary mass of textual commentary the world knows has grown up around it. This commentary has been a stimulus and often a model for all sorts of extrabiblical textual learning, theorizing, and exegesis from Origen through Dante and Milton on to James Joyce and beyond. The title of Northrop Frye's magisterial book, *The Great Code*, a title garnered intertextually from Blake, advertises the unique place of the Bible in the history of interpretation. A code both interprets and itself needs interpretation—as all utterance does, only moreso.

Hermeneutics evolves, and as it evolves today, it grows more aware of orality-literacy contrasts in verbal expression and in noetic processes and of the implications of these contrasts for interpretive study. In it orality and literacy intersect in seemingly the most intensive fashion possible, in the Hebrew scriptures, the Law, the Prophets, and the Writings, and through the Christian books, and most crucially in the gospels.

Paul Ricoeur notes that the Christian kerygma is itself "the rereading of an ancient Scripture" (1980:51). He is referring here, it appears, to the kerygma found in the gospel texts. The gospel text certainly does incorporate an interpretation of the pre-Christian books of the Christian Bible. Northrop Frye insists that in the Christian mind this becomes the chief business of the Old Testament, to illuminate and be illuminated by the New (1982:78–101). But the new interpretation of the pre-Christian books, though it enters into the New Testament texts, was originally and fundamentally not a textual operation, not a text-to-text transaction. Jesus' kerygma, which included, but was not restricted to, an interpretation of the ancient books, was in itself a completely oral event or series of events. (Spoken words are events, not things: they are never present all at once but occur seriatim, syllable-after-syllable.) New Testament texts follow on the oral hermeneutic of Jesus, interpreting his interpretation for textual conveyance.

The involvement of orality in hermeneutic processes was intensive for centuries after Jesus' life on earth and has continued, somewhat abated, to our own time. Although the Bible lies at the heart of Christianity, over the centuries by far most Christians have been illiterate. Until the Protestant Reformation, with its stress on private reading of the scriptures, Christianity had never regarded illiterates as salvifically disadvantaged. In relation to Jesus and before God, they were at least as well off as literates, and maybe better off, for God "singled out the weak of this world to shame the strong" (I Cor. 1:27), though obviously the Christian community needed at least some literates to deal directly with the sacred scriptures and to a degree with certain administrative matters.

Because of the free flow between orality and literacy in the Church, despite the centrality of the biblical text, the full spectrum of interpretive activity in the Church in terms of orality-literacy contrasts is as fascinating as it has been little understood. Once you are aware that oral noetics differ from chirographic noetics, what can you say about what went on, and had to go on, when through the Middle Ages and the Renaissance and later the gospels were interpreted for illiterates by literates—often literates themselves marked by a high residue of orality, not even known to be such? When we add to the hermeneutic perspectives here the further perspective that the gospel itself was a literate interpretation of oral-traditional materials, the questions become even more intriguing. Easy-going categories such as "superstition" or "lack of historical sense," often applied to the illiterate world, appear curiously out of touch with reality. All these new perspectives make the situation much more complex, but also, I believe, far more understandable.

Of course, the reciprocal movement from orality to literacy back to orality and thence to literacy again had, in a dizzying variety of ways, marked the development of the Old Testament, too. For the kind of phenomenon that Kelber discusses in describing Mark's textual reprocessing of oral-traditional performance can be observed in one way or another from Genesis on. Oral materials are textualized, the textual materials then freely circulated orally, with or without some textual control conjoined to oral control, and then are reprocessed from orality into text again. This process is not restricted to religious texts, Christian or Hebrew or other: something like it goes on in ordinary secular learning, particularly in antiquity. The relationship of Aristotle's works, for example, to oral discourse and to texts remains a permanent puzzle: Aristotle at times apparently wrote texts, or perhaps dictated texts or parts of texts, but at other times left behind him only other persons' textualization of his oral performance, perhaps worked over more or less by him (Jaeger, 1948: 168ff).

But in such oral-literate-oral-literate sequences the oral heritage is never so intensive, so professedly integral, or so crucial as in the oral kerygma of Jesus underlying New Testament writings. This kergyma was one person's proclamation in which he incorporated his hermeneutic for an oral-chirographic heritage of a thousand years. Jesus' oral kerygma did not constitute the oral-traditional background of an intellectual elite but rather provided the basic interpretation of existence for an entire community still extant and held together by this kerygma of one who they believed, and still believe, still lives in a transformed, resurrected state. This oral-textual-oral-textual-oral interpretive community is the Church. Other major world religions have an oral-traditional heritage, too, but nothing constituted like this.

In 1974 Avery Dulles published a small, deliberately popularizing, but scholarly and highly informative book, *Models of the Church*, in which he notes that ecclesiologists, Catholic and Protestant, over the years have explained the Christian Church in accord with various models which they had consciously or unconsciously appropriated: the Church has been viewed, variously and in each case inadequately, as an institution, as a mystical communion, as sacrament, as herald, as servant. Dulles notes that other models have been used as well, and states that his selection of these five for study has been made "for simplicity's sake" (1974:9). He suggests that a multiplicity of models is needed to compensate for the limitations sure to mark each and every individual model.

I would suggest that it is possible today to add a further, very helpful model, a model not yet so fully developed as those Dulles considers but now ready for quite full development, that is, a model of the Church as an oral-chirographic interpretive community, founded in oral-traditional materials early interpreted in textual form and thereafter interpreted in a historically continuous communal setting by continuous interaction of the oral and the textual.

A model of the Church as an oral-chirographic interpretive community of the sort suggested here would provide new insights into a great many of the vexing problems centering around the relationship of the Bible and tradition. This relationship has plagued historians and theologians as well as worshiping ecclesial communities over the centuries, but it came to a head with the deep interiorization of literacy and the resulting reorganization of thought processes brought about by print (Ong, 1982:117–138). The Protestant-Catholic division which developed in the wake of typography was marked by a Protestant insistence that Scripture alone (*sola scriptura*) was the source of divine revelation in the Church and the Catholic insistence that, in addition to Scripture, tradition was also a source.

Of course, neither side in the Reformation dispute could be aware of the orality-literacy conflicts at work in the consciousness of the time. Scripture is obviously a literate phenomenon, at least in its terminal phase. Tradition, as Catholics and their opponents understood it and as it has to be understood, involves orality. The Council of Trent (Sess. IV, 8 Apr. 1546) contrasts divine revelation in "written books" (that is, the Bible) and "unwritten traditions" (*sine scripto traditionibus*) which were "received by the Apostles from the mouth of Christ himself" (*ab ipsius Christi ore ab Apostolis acceptae*). Rejecting a proposed draft that divine revelation is contained "partly in the Scriptures and partly in tradition," Trent defined simply that it is contained "in the Scriptures and in unwritten traditions." And yet the explications of Trent's decrees by Renaissance Catholic theologians show the confusions typically deriving from the unexamined bias of the literate mind. Twentieth-century studies have shown how these earlier theologians tended to conceptualize oral tradition itself by implied, and unnoticed, textual analogies, as though tradition itself were a kind of second volume of the Bible which Catholics kept and Protestants had abandoned (Baumgartner, 1953; Burghardt, 1951). Here the same preemptive chirographic mindset evident in Protestant attitudes toward *sola scriptura* manifested itself in a more subtle way. On the other hand, Protestants showed evidence of orality-literacy tensions in counterbalancing their heavy textual investment in *sola scriptura* with a stress on oral preaching that was not foreign to the Catholic tradition but that had never before been quite so strong. These are only samples of the many orality-literacy polarities in the Protestant-Catholic division which call for study.

Our present perspectives for interpreting complex orality-literacy relationships were of course not yet available in Reformation times. The perspectives suggested here have not been available even to present-day scholarship very long. It is not merely that the biblical text is preceded by oral tradition, which the text simply sets down, but that—to take Mark as paradigmatic of all the Gospels and even of all the Bible, though not rigidly so—the biblical text itself comes into being as an interpretation of what went before, the definitive written ecclesial hermeneutic of an original oral kerygma. This does not, of course, at all do away with or compromise Catholic belief as defined by Trent and the First Vatican Council that the Bible is the inspired word of God, having God as its "principal author," but it sets the scene for understanding in greater depth what such belief in divine authorship entails. God works in history—which is what the Incarnation is about. But the work of understanding is just beginning.

Finally, given that biblical hermeneutics has always historically been a major groundbreaker for textual studies generally, secular as well as religious, one can hope that the new orality-literacy perspectives opening on biblical textuality, with the particularly intense focus that biblical textuality has demanded, will also open new insights into many other fields and provide an enlarged understanding of the human condition in its totality which lies at the center of the Bible's own concern.

REFERENCES

Baumgartner, Charles. 1953. "Tradition et magistère," *Recherches de science religeuse*, 41, 161–187.

Burghardt, Walter J. 1951. "The Catholic concept of Tradition," *Proceedings of the Catholic Theological Society of America*, pp. 42–76.

Burton, John. 1977. *The Collection of the Qur'ān*. Cambridge, England: Cambridge University Press.

Dulles, Avery, S. J. 1974. *Models of the Church*. Garden City, N.Y.: Doubleday.

Fish, Stanley. 1980. *Is There a Text in This Class? The Authority of Interpretive Communities*. Cambridge, Mass.: Harvard University Press.

Frye, Northrop. 1982. *The Great Code: The Bible and Literature*. New York and London: Harcourt, Brace, Jovanovich.

Hajnal, István. 1954. *L'enseignement de l'écriture aux universités médiévales*. Budapest: Academia Scientiarum Hungarica Budapestini.

Jaeger, Werner. 1948. *Aristotle: Fundamentals of the History of His Develop-ment*. Trans. with the author's corrections and additions by Richard Robin-son. 2d ed. Oxford: Clarendon Press.

Kelber, Werner H. 1983. *The Oral and the Written Gospel: The Hermeneutics of Speaking and Writing in the Synoptic Tradition, Mark, Paul, and Q*. Phila-delphia: Fortress Press.

O'Keefe, Katherine O'Brien. 1983. "Moths and Mouths: Some Anglo-Saxon Meditations on the Technology of Writing." A paper presented at the General Session on Old English at the Ninety-Eighth Convention of the Modern Language Association of America, December 27–30, 1983, New York, New York.

Ong, Walter J. 1982. *Orality and Literacy: The Technologizing of the Word*. London and New York: Metheun.

Ong, Walter J. 1981. *Fighting for Life: Context, Sexuality, and Consciousness*. Ithaca and London: Cornell University Press.

Ong, Walter J. 1967. *The Presence of the Word*. New Haven and London: Yale University Press.

Ong, Walter J. 1958. *Ramus, Method, and the Decay of Dialogue*. Cambridge, Mass.: Harvard University Press. Paperback 1983.

Peristiany, J. G. (ed.). 1966. *Honor and Shame: The Values of Mediterranean Society*. Chicago: University of Chicago Press.

Ricoeur, Paul. 1980. *Essays on Biblical Interpretation*. Ed. with an introduction by Lewis S. Mudge. Philadelphia: Fortress Press.

Stock, Brian. 1983. *The Implications of Literacy: Written Language and Models of Interpretation in the Eleventh and Twelfth Centuries*. Princeton, N.J.: Princeton University Press.

KELBER'S BREAKTHROUGH

Thomas J. Farrell,
Regis College, Toronto School of Theology

ABSTRACT

The first part of this review essay about *The Oral and the Written Gospel* by Werner H. Kelber explains in some detail the key concepts readers need to understand in order to fully grasp the import of his landmark study: oral-aural communication and primary orality, non-vowelized phonetic alphabetic literacy, vowelized phonetic alphabetic literacy, non-alphabetic writing systems, the sense of time in the primary oral mentality, (alphabetic) textuality, visualism and manuscript culture/mentality, hypervisualism and print culture/mentality, electronically-aided oral-aural awareness and secondary oral culture/mentality, and relationist thinking. The second part of this essay presents a summary of and commentary on each chapter of Kelber's book. The third part offers an assessment of the larger implications of his study for our deeper understanding of the orientation of Christianity.

0.1 Walter J. Ong, S.J., has devoted the better part of his scholarly career to investigating the psychodynamics of primary orality and alphabetic literacy in chirographic and typographic forms and secondary electronically-accentuated contemporary orality. His magnificent phenomenological account of psychocultural historical development is elaborated in several hundred essays and reviews, some of which have been collected for publication as books, while others are themselves book-length essays. His distinguished scholarly work led to his being elected president of the Modern Language Association of America for 1978. Somewhat earlier in his career he was invited to present a paper at the plenary session of the American Academy of Religion in St. Louis on October 29, 1976, in which paper he made the following observation:

> Everyone in or near scriptural studies today is in some way aware that the Bible in great part comes out of an oral tradition, and in

> various ways, although scriptural scholarship as a whole, so far as
> I can see, still shows little awareness in depth of the psycho-
> dynamics of an oral culture as these psychodynamics have been
> worked out by Albert B. Lord and Eric A. Havelock and some
> others, so that the definitive breakthrough in scriptural studies, I
> believe, is yet to come. (Ong, 1977:231)

In *The Oral and the Written Gospel*, Werner H. Kelber ably begins to
work out the psychodynamics of primary orality and of textuality in the
gospel tradition, and in my estimate he does achieve the definitive
breakthrough in biblical studies for which Father Ong has been waiting.
0.2   The Bible is essentially the product of the primary oral mentality
described by Ong (1967, 1971, 1977, 1982a), Havelock (1963, 1978, 1982),
Lord (1960), and others (see Foley, 1985 for notations of around 1800
studies in some 90 language areas; Maxwell, 1983). In other words, the
thought and expression recorded in the Bible, while divinely inspired,
manifest the psychodynamics of primary orality, as do all early, pre-
philosophic writings. I for one wish that Professor Kelber had made this
point clearer in his treatment of the gospel tradition. Even if he had,
however, he probably would not have avoided thereby being misunderstood by print-oriented biblical scholars such as Raymond E. Brown,
S.S., who do not yet understand the sophisticated analysis of primary
orality employed by Kelber. For even after I pointed out to Father Brown
that he does not understand the concepts concerning primary orality
(Farrell, 1984), he responded that he does, but he manifestly demonstrated by what he says in his response to me that he actually does not
understand the complex concepts employed by Kelber (Brown, 1984). Of
course, I recognize that Father Brown has made an invaluable contribution to biblical scholarship, but with all due respect for his own achievement I wish to point out that he simply does not understand the concepts
derived from orality-literacy studies. The concepts do need to be carefully understood. Consequently, I propose to explain them in some detail
before I consider Kelber's book in detail.
1.0   Ong describes four major psychocultural stages of development,
and Northrop Frye (1982) in effect describes the language orientation
(language in the sense of *langage*, as distinct from *langue*) in the first
three epochs identified by Ong: metaphoric language is characteristic of
primary oral culture (which is innocent of reading and writing);
metonymic language is characteristic of literate culture in the manuscript
stage of development, from ancient Greece through medieval Europe
("literate" in the sense of using vowelized phonetic alphabetic writing);
and descriptive language is characteristic of literate culture in the print
stage. Frye speculates that a new stage of language may be emerging now
in what Ong calls our secondary oral stage of culture, which grows out of

it and is rooted in literacy. (A caveat needs to be noted here: Ong [1982a:83–93] contends that non-alphabetic writing systems such as syllabic and pictographic writing systems do not transform thinking as phonetic alphabetic writing systems do, and so cultures in which those writing systems are central are residual forms of primary oral culture.) However that may be, the sensitive study of the psychodynamics of primary orality is undoubtedly fostered by secondary orality. Conversely the mentality of print culture as manifested either in Protestants, Jews, Catholics, Anglicans or non-believers who study the Bible does not foster the deep understanding of primary orality made possible in secondary oral culture in its most sophisticated scholarly works.

1.1. The primary oral mentality is accurately characterized by other scholars in terms other than Frye's term "metaphoric." Havelock (1963) characterizes it as using imagistic thinking which is action-oriented. In *Orality and Literacy*, Ong refers to it as employing concrete operational thinking because the conceptualizations used tend to be concrete. (The concrete operational thinking developed in primary oral culture is probably somewhat different from the concrete operational thinking described by Jean Piaget, because the subjects he studied grew up in an essentially literate culture. Consequently, when other researchers such as T. Kellaghan (1968) and A. Heron and W. Dowel (1974) report that certain elements of concrete operational thinking as described by Piaget do not occur in certain other subjects, it can be inferred that those subjects probably grew up in a residual form of primary oral culture. Similarly, when Arthur R. Jensen calls attention to the fact that black children in the United States of America score significantly lower than white children on measures of abstract thinking, it can be argued that this difference is due to the fact that the abstract thinking of literacy has not yet been fully assimilated into ghetto black culture, which is largely a residual form of primary oral culture [Farrell, 1983].) In *The Savage Mind*, Claude Levi-Strauss describes the primary oral mentality as totalizing, and in *Sacred Discontent*, Herbert N. Schneidau describes it as mythologizing. No doubt other terms have been used to accurately describe various dimensions of the primary oral mentality, and no doubt others will be introduced in future studies.

1.2 The claims about literacy and textuality also need to be carefully understood. Havelock and Ong use the term "literacy" to refer to both non-vowelized phonetic alphabetic writing and vowelized phonetic alphabetic writing. Havelock (1982) argues that the use of vowelized phonetic alphabetic writing was related to the development of abstract thinking in ancient Greece. Now, twentieth century schooling in the West is essentially schooling in literacy and literate modes of thought, just as the development of literate modes of thought with the aid of the vowelized phonetic alphabet in ancient Greece was in effect schooling.

Thus A. R. Luria's (1976) field study of schooled and unschooled peasants
in rural Russia supports Havelock's claim that literacy is related to the
development of abstract thinking. Likewise, the report of Sylvia Scribner
and Michael Cole (1981) about the Vai schoolchildren in English-language
school in Liberia supports Havelock's claim, whereas their report about
the Vai adults who had studied English in school, years before Scribner
and Cole did their field study, suggests that either those men simply did
not learn abstract thinking in school (just as many ghetto black children
attend school without learning abstract thinking) or they had simply
forgotten in the intervening years what they may have learned earlier
(just as many ghetto black children "forgot" what they had learned
ostensibly in intensive Upward Bound programs in the sixties, as indicated by the "backsliding" of their scores on mental measures after they
left the programs and re-assimilated the patterns of thought and expression of the residual form of primary oral culture in which they lived).
Scribner and Cole also report that subjects who had studied modern
Arabic in school did not develop abstract thinking. Of course, the two
explanations just mentioned may explain their non-development, but a
third explanation is also possible in this case. In a lecture at the international colloquium on literacy at the University of Toronto on March 9,
1985, Derrick de Kerckhove noted that modern Arabic uses a non-
vowelized alphabet. Consequently, the Scribner and Cole report that
those schooled in modern Arabic do not develop abstract thinking may
support another aspect of Havelock's work—that vowelized rather than
non-vowelized writing is related to the development of abstract thinking.
However that may be, the quality that Schneidau variously calls de-
mythologizing, self-criticism, and alienation did develop with the use of
non-vowelized phonetic alphabetic writing in ancient Israel. Kelber bor-
rows the term "distanciation" from Paul Ricoeur to designate this quality,
and uses the technical term "textuality" to refer to the effects of tran-
scribing primary oral thought and expression in phonetic writing of
either the non-vowelized or the vowelized kind. Kelber, in accord with
Schneidau's analysis, claims that distanciation develops with textuality.
1.21 Two points need to be very carefully noted here. First, Schneidau
clearly believes that this quality did not develop in non-Western cultures
(such as Arabic culture) that had non-vowelized writing. If that claim is
true, then non-vowelized phonetic alphabetic writing needs to be considered to be a necessary but not sufficient condition for the development of
this quality in ancient Israel. However, if the quality of distanciation
developed elsewhere where non-vowelized phonetic alphabetic writing
was used, then this kind of writing system may be not only the necessary
but perhaps the sufficient condition for the development of this quality.
Of course, the contention here is that this quality of distanciation would
not develop with non-alphabetic writing systems such as syllabic or

pictographic writing systems. Second, whereas Schneidau is referring to the textualization of the Old Testament in the non-vowelized ancient Hebrew, Kelber is referring to the textualization of the gospel tradition in the vowelized ancient Greek. If the use of vowelized ancient Greek were a sufficient condition for the development of abstract thinking, then one might reasonably expect to find abstract thinking in the New Testament. But Frye in effect notes that the language of the Bible is characterized by the concrete operational thinking of primary orality, not by the abstractions and rational argumentation of the abstract thinking of vowelized phonetic alphabetic literacy:

> There are no true rational arguments in the Bible, not even in the New Testament, which despite its late date keeps very close to the Old Testament in its attitude toward language. What may look like rational argument, such as the Epistle to the Hebrews, turns out on closer analysis to be a disguised form of exhortation. Nor is there much functional use of abstraction. Biblical Hebrew is an almost obsessively concrete language, and while there are a few abstract terms like 'nature' in the New Testament, they hardly affect what is still a metaphorical structure. (Frye, 1982:27)[1]

Karl Barth in effect also identifies the Bible with primary orality when he says, "And so the Bible is not a philosophic book, but . . . the book of God's mighty acts . . ." (Barth, 1959:38). For, as Havelock notes, the primary oral mentality is action-oriented, not abstraction-oriented as is the fully literate mentality, and so a book about God's mighty acts is especially attuned to the primary oral mentality. In other words, neither the Old nor the New Testaments are products of the kind of abstract thinking Havelock associates with the mature development of vowelized literacy. Since the gospel tradition was transcribed in ancient Greek, ancient Greek is not a sufficient condition for the development of abstract thinking, although it may be, as Havelock in effect contends, a necessary condition. However that may be, the fact that the gospel writings are not characterized by abstract thinking does not mean that there were no other effects associated with their written composition. Whatever those effects may be are attributed by Kelber to textualization in phonetic alphabetic writing. Thus Kelber uses the shorthand expression "textuality" to distinguish the effects of concern to him in his study from the effects Havelock associates with the mature development of vowelized literacy.

1.3 Now, if one grants the essential correctness of Ong's analysis of psychocultural history as summarized above, then one would also have to allow that a distinctive approach to interpreting reality may occur in primary oral culture, manuscript culture, print culture, and secondary oral culture. Following such a supposition, one might turn to an anthropological study of a living but dying primary oral culture such as *Bemba Myth and Ritual: The Impact of Literacy on an Oral Culture* by Kevin B. Maxwell, S.J., to discern some characteristics of the primary oral mentality that might enable a fresh understanding of some biblical data. Maxwell has sensitively analyzed the culture of the Bemba people in rural northeastern Zambia. The most important finding in his report concerns the primary oral sense of time:

> Time for the Bemba is conceived as a meaningful cluster of concrete events and activities. Because the Bemba live existentially in and for the present, their language reckons time around the present. It refers to 'near present' and 'further from the present,'. . . . The distant past and future are not really significant categories. The tense of a verb is more intent on determining whether a sequence of events is *complete* or incomplete, hence *perfect* or imperfect. . . . (Emphasis his; Maxwell, 1983:90)

Maxwell goes on to explain that the Bemba manifest no true sense of the past as past, and R. A. F. MacKenzie, S.J., says that virtually the same thing is true of the ancient Hebrews (lecture, Regis College, October 15, 1984). I would say that this is true of all people in primary oral culture. For the sense of the past as past arises with the mature development of vowelized literacy, as in Plato's nostalgia for the "past" Socrates, but the sense of the past as past begins to become widespread and commonplace only with the development of modern scientific history in the seventeenth century—in other words, in print culture. The parts of the past that the Bemba retain in their living human memory carry some lesson for the present. Even though the verbs indicate completed action, the time and situation represented are not so much the past as past, as a kind of ideal time and situation. Maxwell notes that "the past" is used by the Bemba as a metaphor for "the ideal" (Maxwell, 1983:90). A similar point can be made about biblical Greek. Maximillian Zerwick, S.J. (1963: 77–99) in discussing the so-called tenses of biblical Greek notes that some "tenses" do not even express the notion of time. Specifically, the aorist "connotes simply the action without further determination." In other words, the aorist does not express the sense of the past as past, but calls attention to an ideal of some kind. I would suggest that the seeming past is used in many passages in the Bible to express an ideal of some kind.

1.31   For example, the oral-traditional story of the fall in the past in the Book of Genesis may very well express in reverse, so to speak, the ideal of man moving from the sufferings of this life upwards to God in a paradisal (ideal) spiritual union. According to David L. Fleming, S.J., Pierre Teilhard de Chardin, S.J., intuitively grasped just this point:

> For [Teilhard] sees a deeper meaning in the persons of Adam and
> Eve; they are symbols of mankind moving Godwards. Eden is
> salvation constantly offered to all, refused by many, and attained
> by man in unity with Jesus Christ. (Fleming, 1969:123)

In other words, only the hypervisualist print mentality, as Ong styles it,
could mistake Genesis for a modern scientific treatise about the creation
and evolution of the cosmos and man (the name "Adam" no doubt means
"mankind"). For the print mentality tends to be exceedingly literalist (or
descriptive, as Frye puts it) in its interpretation of the Bible. Of course,
this same tendency leads to the development of modern scientific history, as mentioned above, and of modern science. However, the tendency of people in print culture to interpret biblical data descriptively
leads to a more literalist reading than what prevailed in the preceding
manuscript culture, which fostered a fourfold consideration of the literal,
allegorical, moral, and anagogical dimensions of biblical data. Moreover,
the pronounced literalist tendency of the print mentality is strikingly
different from the metaphoric orientation, as Frye puts it, of the primary
oral mentality. Considered within the context of a metaphoric orientation, the Genesis accounts of creation are metaphoric expressions of
man's dependence on God (imaged by creation itself) and of man's need
to strive in the present, even in the midst of the terrors of history, to draw
closer to God. The need to draw closer is imaged in reverse by the fall,
and the desirability of drawing closer to God is imaged by the ideal of
Eden, as Fleming notes. Contrary to a literal reading of the Genesis
account of the fall, even as seemingly implied in Romans 5.12 and 1
Corinthians 15.22, this interpretation of Genesis accentuates that man in
his "original" (natural) human condition is not yet fully united with God
and thus tends to sin. But man is free to turn to God and be saved, by
turning away from sin (the forbidden fruit). United with God, men may
overcome the tendency to sin and live a fruitful good life (imaged by the
tree of life). Since Adam and Even cannot seriously be considered to have
been real historical human beings who actually lived in the past, this
highly Christian interpretation denies the historicity of Adam and Eve,
re-mythologizes them as it were, and emphasizes that the point of the
story (or myth) is to call attention to man's sinful condition and the need
to turn to God.

1.32   Another example of the primary oral use of the past to image an
ideal occurs in Isaiah 1.21:

> How the faithful city
>   has become a harlot,
>   she that was full of justice!

> Righteousness lodged in her,
> but not murderers.

Since the actual past of Jerusalem was never full of justice, this is probably an instance of the past tense being used to refer to an ideal, an ideal which happens to coincide in essence with the paradisal ideal just discussed, even though different images are used. No doubt other examples could be found in the Bible of the past tense being used to refer to an ideal situation or state. Moreover, Maxwell's observation about the future not being a significant category in the Bemba language in the sense of *langue* may also be very important for understanding the language in the sense of *langage* of primary orality, even in the residual form of primary orality found in the New Testament. Consider, for example, the further implications of this for understanding the various comments about the future coming of the parousia. These various points suggest some possible implications of studies of primary orality for biblical studies beyond the implications already developed by Kelber and other biblical scholars cited by John Miles Foley (1985).

1.33   Now the full text of Barth's sentence from which the above-quoted words were taken needs to be carefully reconsidered: "And so the Bible is not a philosophical book, but a history book, the book of God's mighty acts, in which God becomes knowable by us" (1959:38). The Bible is concerned with acts, for the primary oral mentality is action-oriented, not oriented toward the use of abstractions in rational argumentation. But the Bible is not a history book in the modern sense, even when historical events may have contributed to the making of the biblical narratives. For even the historically-based narratives were not intended to be historical in the modern sense of the term, because the primary oral mentality used the past (the historical element) to express what Bruno Bettelheim (1976:37, 39) calls a superego-ideal. This is even true of the four evangelists. The four gospels are not history in the modern sense of the term. The modern sense of history developed with the sense of the past as past fostered by print culture. The gospels do not express a sense of the past as past because they are the products of the primary oral mentality which simply had not yet developed a sense of the past as past. Of course, the gospels use the past, but the narratives involving historical elements are not aptly characterized as history, just as the stories of creation in Genesis are not aptly characterized as science. Nevertheless, the biblical narratives can help us know how God becomes knowable by us, as Barth suggests.   .

1.34   Since the influence of primary orality on the composition of all four gospels is being stressed here, some possible arguments concerning the influence of non-vowelized or vowelized literacy need to be considered. Some people who identify linearity with literacy may argue that insofar as the four gospels are linear, they are to that extent literate. But events in time actually do occur one before and another after, and the mere oral-parataxic chronicling of events would yield a seemingly linear narrative. For example, the story of the Mandinka people told to Alex Haley when he was in search of the roots of his ancestor of two centuries ago, Kunta Kinte, followed an apparently linear sequence by simply employing the oral technique of parataxis (concerning the parataxis of primary orality, see Notopoulos 1949 and Perry 1937). Of course, the *Iliad* and the *Odyssey* and no doubt many other epics out of oral tradition start in the middle of things (as does Mark's gospel). But they do so not out of "oral necessity" but out of a sense of artistry. Moreover, the most important thing to note is that they are plotted like a Chinese puzzle with boxes within boxes (Ong 1982: 27, 195). Not surprisingly, Charles H. Lohr's (1961) study shows that Matthew's gospel follows such an organizational pattern. Most likely the other three gospels also follow that kind of pattern of organization, regardless of their seeming linearity. Further-more, if one assumes that the author of Matthew's gospel had known Mark's gospel and wanted to supplement it, then one would argue that as a primary oral composer the evangelist would add only "boxed" mate-rial—only material which was structurally counterbalanced by other material in the "boxed" position. Therefore, if the author of Matthew's gospel planned to add material to expand the ending of Mark's gospel, he would have to expand the beginning of his gospel by adding material to set up the "box." For only by doing so would he be able to satisfy the primary oral sense of balance. Of course, the same would be true for the author of Luke's gospel. Now, since Candi Rureke's recently transcribed and translated performance of the Mwindo epic begins with the episode about the birth of the hero (Biebuyck and Mateene 1969: 41–60), it is not plausible to argue that primary oral people would never begin a story with the birth of the hero and that only people influenced by literacy and its linearity would begin the story of a hero with the beginning of the hero's life at birth. Consequently, it would not be surprising to find that the then living oral tradition about Jesus contained anecdotal material about his infancy and childhood for the authors of Matthew and Luke to appropriate for use in their projected expanded gospels. After all, if they were going to expand their accounts of Jesus' end, they may have been attracted to available material about the beginning and early life of Jesus out of their sense of the need to counterbalance the endings of their accounts at the beginning to establish the "box." In short, the seeming linearity of the four gospels may not indicate any influence from literacy, since the techniques of primary oral composition could adequately ac-count for the seeming linearity. However, another possible influence of vowelized literacy needs to be considered with respect to the fourth gospel in particular. Some people who identify abstract thinking with vowelized literacy may argue that the "Logos" in the prologue is an abstract idea and conclude that this shows the influence of vowelized literacy on the fourth gospel. Now, since the "days" in the first half of the fourth gospel echo the seven (oral-parataxically ordered) "days" of creation in Genesis, the evangelist clearly had Genesis on his mind when he composed the fourth gospel. Moreover, he could have come to the insights expressed in the prologue by pondering the accounts of creation in Genesis. In other words, the Genesis accounts of creation could have led him to consider the question of what the God who creates ·by speaking speaks when he creates. The mere use of concrete thinking in terms of the analogy with human speaking would suffice to give him the Logos of the prologue as the answer to the question about what God speaks. In short, the abstract thinking of vowelized literacy need not necessarily have been in play at all for the evangelist to have composed any part of the prologue to the fourth gospel. Be that as it may, another argument against the possible influence of vowelized literacy on the four gospels deserves to be mentioned. The sense of the past as past appears to be connected with vowelized literacy. By contrast, the use of selected elements from the past in primary oral narratives seems to have nothing to do with nostalgia for the past. Instead, it grows out of the need for what Bettelheim calls a superego-ideal which presumably helps encourage people in the present to struggle with the trials of life. The four gospels do not express a sense of nostalgia about the Jesus of the past, as Plato does about the Socrates of the past, nor do they express a sense of the past as past. In short, the four gospels do not show the influence of vowelized literacy.[2]

1.4   As I just indicated in passing, Ong's work also enables us to understand the history of biblical interpretation more fully, for it follows from his insights that distinctive interpretive approaches emerge with the visualism of manuscript culture and the hypervisualism of print culture, as literacy and the mentality it fosters come to be interiorized more and more, as he puts it. Since secondary orality presumably counterbalances the hypervisualism fostered by print culture, perhaps it is worth mentioning that in *Christ and Apollo,* William F. Lynch, S.J. argues for a contemporary appropriation of the fourfold approach to interpretation developed in manuscript culture, which approach considers the literal, allegorical, moral, and anagogical meanings of biblical data. The fact that such a sophisticated critic advocates this fourfold approach suggests that the sensibility/mentality fostered by secondary orality may be deeply attuned to the manuscript mentality, in addition to being open to a critical appreciation of the primary oral as well as the print mentality. Of course, the fourfold medieval approach to interpreting biblical data was supplanted historically by interpretive strategies attuned to the hypervisualism of the print mentality. Here Ong's (1958) work on Peter Ramus (1515–1572) is instructive for understanding Ong's relationist account of these complex changes in sensibility/mentality. For Ong identifies Peter of Spain (born between 1210 and 1215; died 1277) and Rudolph Agricola (1444–1485) as precursors of this paragon of the print mentality, even though they lived before the movable printing press became popular. In a similar way, even though Martin Luther's (1483–1546) formative years were perhaps free from the direct impact of the printing press, he undoubtedly represents the print mentality's descriptive approach, as Frye puts it, to interpreting the Bible. If it is accurate to associate Luther with the literalist tendency of interpretation identified above with the print mentality, then this association nicely illustrates what Ong styles a relationist analysis of events. In the case of the print mentality, a certain kind of sensibility had to emerge in order for the movable printing press to emerge, and yet once the printing press emerged, it fostered the further development of the sensibility/mentality that had made it possible. In other words, the emergence of what Ong calls a hypervisual sensibility was related to the development of the printing press, and the printing press in turn was related to the spread of hypervisualism. Thus the printing press was a necessary but not sufficient condition for the spread of hypervisualism. If we were to speak of Luther as representing early hypervisualism, then we would be able to range later interpreters down to contemporaries on a continuum of hypervisualist development from him. In a recent spirited review essay in *The Heythrop Journal*, Frans Jozef van Beeck, S.J., calls attention to the parallel hypervisualist tendencies in Catholic theology and in effect points out that the call of the Second Vatican Council for a dialogic orientation in theology is deeply attuned to the sensibility/mentality of secondary orality. Paradoxically, the print mentality did eventually culminate in the development of the sensibility/mentality associated by Ong with secondary orality, for the scientific and technological mentality fostered by print culture led to a series of electronic inventions that in turn have re-accentuated oral-aural orientations in secondary oral culture. The sophisticated secondary oral mentality is sensitive to the presuppositions of the print mentality and is able to describe and assess the salient features of not only the primary oral mentality, the manuscript mentality, and the print mentality, but also the secondary oral mentality, as Ong has done so ably. While Foley (1985) has conveniently pulled together and annotated biblical studies by Charles H. Lohr and numerous others attuned to the influence of primary orality, which studies are as such a manifestation of the growth of the sophisticated secondary oral mentality, Kelber's *Oral and Written Gospel* is the greatest effort to date to overcome the presuppositions of the print mentality and to analyze biblical data in the fresh light of studies of primary orality and textuality.

2.0 In chapter one of *The Oral and the Written Gospel*, Kelber uses studies of primary orality to call into question Rudolf Bultmann's model

of evolutionary progression of the synoptic tradition and Birger
Gerhardsson's model of passive transmission. He nicely sums up his
findings in three points:

> In the first place, both dismiss the relevance of a differentiated
> treatment of orality versus textuality. Media differences are
> blurred or belittled in regard to synoptic processes. Second, each
> postulates a single directional course of transmission. Although
> both scholars acknowledge a predominantly oral phase of synoptic
> tradition, each chooses to reduce the dynamics of living words to
> the straight path of linearity. Third, both assume a smooth transit
> from oral transmission to gospel composition, and likewise regard
> the gospel as being in unbroken continuity with its oral precur-
> sors. For Bultmann, the gospel is the expected result of pre-
> gospel processes, and for Gerhardsson the gospel's genetic code
> has been inscribed into tradition at its very inception. (Kelber,
> 1983:32)

In sum, Kelber identifies the failure to treat orality as a medium in its
own right and apart from textuality as the root cause ". . . for the imposi-
tion of linearity upon oral life and the trivialization of the genesis of
Mark" (Kelber, 1983:32).
2.1   Since Kelber is also the author of *The Kingdom of Mark* and *Mark's
Story of Jesus,* perhaps it is not surprising that two of the five chapters in
his new book are exclusively about Mark, while the remaining two are as
much about Mark as about Paul and other matters related to the synoptic
tradition. In chapter two, Kelber considers Mark's oral legacy. He identifies three kinds of discourse in Mark: ordering discourse, disordering
discourse, and discourse that could be interpreted as either ordering or
disordering discourse. I would point out that the ordering discourse is to
prepare for and point toward the so-called disordering discourse, and for
that reason I prefer to refer to the latter as re-ordering or transforming
discourse. Kelber's category of ordering discourse in Mark includes what
he styles heroic stories and polarization stories. Now, Lord in *The Singer
of Tales* establishes that episodes in oral stories follow formulary patterns,
and Kelber identifies the formulary patterns of these two kinds of stories.
The ten healing stories, which he styles heroic, proceed through the
pattern of the exposition of the healing, the performance of the healing,
and the confirmation of the healing, with typical but varied elements in
each of these three movements of each story. Kelber also identifies the
basic pattern and the variable elements in the three exorcism stories in
Mark, which he styles polarization stories. In the heroic and the polarization stories Jesus acts as an ordering presence, and so these stories are
part of the category that Kelber calls ordering discourse. The six identi-
fiable parabolic stories in Mark fit into Kelber's category of disordering

discourse. Kelber regards the parable as a quintessential form of primary oral speech, and he notes that the parables as metaphors invite poly-valent hearings: "The parabolist does not entirely say what he means and mean what he says" (Kelber, 1983:74). The five didactic stories in Mark exhibit some of the qualities of so-called disordering discourse, depend-ing on how they are interpreted. Kelber points out that the disciples of Jesus are to learn how to interpret what I call the reordering discourse by following in the way of Jesus.

2.2   Having described Mark's manifold oral legacy in chapter two, Kel-ber in chapter three considers the gospel of Mark as textuality. After he nicely summarizes the central argument of Havelock's *Preface to Plato*, he suggests that the disciples' learning from Jesus is an instance of the oral mimesis which Plato attacks (e.g., in *Ion*) and that Jesus' rebuking the disciples for their lack of comprehension shows that the oral mimesis did not work. But I would point out that the disciples did perform exorcisms and miracles of healing. And so did other prophets who used the name of Jesus as Kelber notes in his discussion of Mark 13. Shouldn't we then say that the oral mimesis worked on the level of ordering discourse?

Might we not then say that Jesus was rebuking the disciples because they had not moved to the level of re-ordered or transformed discourse (or consciousness)? My distinction here is pertinent to Kelber's argu-ment, for he argues in effect that composing for writing transforms consciousness away from oral mimesis. Since composing for writing involves distanciation, Kelber uses Mark 13 to argue that Mark wanted to distance himself from the oral mimesis of the prophetic Jesus in order to reflect on the words and deeds of Jesus in a new and deeper way, a way fostered by composing for writing and a way presumably consonant with Jesus' rebukes. Composing for writing, Kelber in effect claims, enabled Mark to move away from the oral sense of immediate (close) presence associated with the prophets mentioned in Mk. 13 to a stress on the absence of the living Lord and the mysterious history of the kingdom. Kelber argues that composing for writing is equivalent to a re-ordering of oral tradition because ". . . the faculty of writing to apportion items along the artificial construct of the straight line forces a systematic ordering upon language unknown to spoken words" (Kelber, 1983:107), and in the case of Mark, Kelber points out, this is connected with a denigration of mimetic oral order and an accentuation of Jesus' re-ordering discourse. Even though Mark moves from orality to textuality the imagistic lan-guage of orality persists in what he has had transcribed. But Kelber suggests that the imagistic language itself is transformed into more obviously metaphorical language. For example, the miracle stories are not just vivid images of actions but also metaphors for the kingdom. Kelber's carefully nuanced analysis here is consonant with both Frye's and Havelock's descriptions of primary oral language, even though Kelber is pointing out a subtle shift that occurs when it is transformed by textuality. I would point out that Kelber does not claim that the language of biblical textuality becomes what Frye describes as metonymic language, nor does he claim that it becomes what Havelock describes as abstract thinking—both of which are associated with the mature development of vowelized phonetic alphabetic literacy. But the textuality of the gospel, Kelber claims, leads to a sense of language that is different from the mimetic orientation of primary orality.

2.3   In chapter four, Kelber considers orality and textuality in Paul. He insightfully discusses Paul's seeming antitheses of Law and faith, on the one hand, and letter and Spirit, on the other hand. I would point out that there is a definite parallel between the ordering discourse in Mark and the discussion of Law and the letter in Paul and between the re-ordering discourse in Mark and the discussion of faith and spirit in Paul. The former in each pair both involve a dying to self in order to establish order, and so they are analogous to Jesus' death. The latter both involve a new form of life, and so they are analogous to Jesus' resurrection. The pattern that I am pointing out here is consonant with the pattern of deathly-crucible-followed-by-new-life that Frye points out in his treatment of Jonah and Job.

2.4   In chapter five, Kelber suggests that the written gospel is a counter-form to, rather than an extension of, oral hermeneutics. He calls attention to the relative paucity of oral forms in the passion narrative and suggests that the distance fostered by composing for writing was necessary for the passion narrative even to be composed:

> The Jesus who performs deeds of power invites oral remembering, and the heroic and polarization stories appeal to mythopoetic identification. The Jesus who dies in powerlessness is the antihero. If the antihero is to become an attractive figure, distance from and skepticism toward oral clichés is indispensable. Freed from the obligation to shape knowledge in memorable forms and figures, writing can overcome orality's entrenched heroism and cultivate an alternative philosophy. (Kelber, 1983:197)

There is a point to what Kelber says, but I would challenge what he says to a certain extent. Is Jesus an antihero? In *Orality and Literacy*, Ong describes the antihero: ". . . the antihero, who, instead of facing up to the foe, constantly turns tail and runs away, as [does] the protagonist in John Updike's *Rabbit Run*" (Ong, 1982a: 70). Jesus did not turn tail and run away; so I do not consider him to be an antihero. Moreover, his passion is an extraordinary event, not an ordinary one, and oral memorability gravitates towards extraordinary actions. Furthermore, he laid down his life for others, which amounts to almost a definition of a hero. But these qualifications do not argue against Kelber's basic conclusion: ". . . when the written medium took full control, [Jesus was transformed from] the speaker of kingdom parables into the parable of the kingdom of God" (Kelber, 1983:220). "The parable," says Kelber, "seeks direct engagement with hearers who continue the process initiated by the story. But as it withholds meaning, reveals and conceals simultaneously, the parable feeds on the very distanciation that typifies writing. . . . Parables, we repeat, are unfinished stories, and whether they are being heard or read, they are contingent on the work of cocreators" (Kelber, 1983:218). Kelber's work leads him to suggest that the gospel belongs to the parable genre, and so we end up with the gospel-as-written squarely in the domain of what Frye calls metaphorical language and calling for an oral-participatory response to the presence of the Word.[3]

3.0 But to what are Christians called in our work as cocreators? To cocreate specifically Christian heroism, I would suggest. For to die to one's discomforts by loving another as one loves oneself, with the aid of the grace of Jesus Christ, in the ordinary interactions of daily life is indeed heroic. Moreover, since reflective people are encouraged to keep up the good fight by the inspiration of heroic examples, heroism in ordinary things is required in order for Christians to be the light of the world. Furthermore, the life and death and resurrection and ascension of Jesus Christ—in others words, all the events in his story considered together—are neither essentially tragic nor essentially comic: not tragic because his efforts were not wasted, even though he died (just as Beowulf died in the heroic act of saving his people, as Maurice B. McNamee, S.J., insightfully notes in his study of *Honor and the Epic Hero*); not comic because the resurrection and ascension were not simply reassuring and encouraging, but wonder- and joy-filling historical events overriding the comic and tragic dimensions of his life (given the nature of the primary oral mentality as textualized in the New Testament, I do not doubt the historicity of those two events). If Christians are called to follow the way of his life, that is a call to a heroic orientation to life. As McNamee points out in his study of heroism, three points formulated by Thomas Aquinas can be appropriated to delineate what is necessary for Christ-like heroism in the ordinary acts of one's life: (1) one must acknowledge that the gifts one has come from God; (2) one must deliberately choose to use one's gifts to serve others as well as oneself out of one's love for God (as distinct from the willy-nilly serving of others that is an inevitable aspect of being social); and (3) one must acknowledge the role of divine providence in any good one helps, as cocreator, bring about and therefore thank God.

3.1 If the story of Jesus is a heroic story designed to encourage his followers to engage freely and even joyfully in ordinary acts of heroic love, then some other very important things about the gospel tradition can be more fully understood. Kelber points out elsewhere in this volume that the four canonical gospels are narratives, whereas The Gospel of Thomas is only a semi-narrativized collection of sayings. He implies that narrative as such helped communicate something essential about the message of Jesus. Now, Ong (1982b:3) notes that narrative organizes experience and consciousness. If the message of Jesus is that his followers are to live heroic lives, as one in effect would by following not only his sayings but also the example of his life, then narratives, which register his experience and consciousness, are much more likely to communicate this message than would a semi-narrativized collection of his sayings. For the narrative episodes of the canonical gospels show him in action, in accord with the dictates of the primary oral mentality, and these narrative episodes remind the followers of Jesus Christ that they are to show themselves to be his followers in action. Of course, Kelber is undoubtedly correct in saying that our actions need to be reflectively considered. For it is only through reflectively considered acts that people actuate their freedom (unreflective acts grow out of impulse or perhaps habit), and it is only through our free acts that we come to realize our individual uniqueness, as Jesus himself did in freely accepting his own death rather than turning tail and running from his captors. From freely accepted acts of love done out of love for God, Christians hope to become the light of the world and be known by others for their unique goodness, just as Jesus was and is known by others for his own unique goodness in freely accepting to die for our salvation from sin out of his love for God and us. Ong has aptly summed up the orientation I am here styling Christian heroism:

> All of us want to realize ourselves as distinct persons, but we also want others—lots of others—to know that we are our own distinct selves. We do not want to be unique all alone. (Ong, 1982b:3–4)

Of course, people can be known for their wickedness rather than for their goodness, in which case their being known amounts to being infamous. But Christians are called upon to be known for their goodness, in which case their being known amounts to being famous, at least within the scope of people among whom they are known. Thus Christian heroism in ordinary acts is integrally connected with establishing one's good name and thereby winning fame to a certain degree for one's cocreation of goodness in this world.

NOTES

[1] Of course, one could argue that there is a certain kind of rationality to biblical thought. Frye no doubt would grant this, although he would say that this kind of rationality is not what he

means by rational argumentation. I would say that the biblical kind of rationality (and all other primary oral rationality) is the rationality of concrete operational thinking and that the kind of rationality Frye refers to as rational argumentation is the rationality of abstract (or literate) thinking. If I were to appropriate Mortimer J. Adler's (1982) distinction between perceptual thought and conceptual thought, I would say that oral (concrete operational) thought and literate (abstract) thought are kinds of conceptual thought, as distinct from perceptual thought.

[2] Someone might object that Odysseus, who presumably represent the primary oral mentality, feels a strong sense of nostalgia for his family and home and that his nostalgia for the past is not necessarily associated with literacy. But the story of Odysseus as we have it does not show that he had a sense of the people of his past comparable to Plato's sense of the Socrates of his past. Even so, someone else might object that even the kind of nostalgia expressed by Odysseus in his desire to return to Ithaca shows the nostalgia characteristic of literacy and that this demonstrates the influence of literacy on the characterization of Odysseus. This objection amounts to saying that the difference between the nostalgia of Odysseus and of Plato differ in degree, not in kind. My response to this objection is the same as my response to the other objection: that the nostalgia expressed by each of them differ in kind, not merely in degree. The readers will have to adjudicate this matter for themselves. However, it is worth mentioning that the Homeric story sounds like a cathartic, so to speak, for the kind of nostalgia experienced by Odysseus during his odyssey, whereas the Platonic dialogues sound like a glorification of the past as past.

[3] The author wishes to thank the editors of *Cross Currents* for permission to use material in this review essay that was originally published in a slightly different version in *Cross Currents* 35 (1985): 350–352. In addition, the author wishes to thank David M. Stanley, S.J., for his helpful comments on this essay.

Works Consulted

Adler, Mortimer J.
   1982   "Minds and Brains: Angels, Humans, and Brutes." The 1982 Harvey Cushing Oration. *Journal of Neurosurgery* 57: 309–15.

Barth, Karl
   1959   *Dogmatics in Outline.* Trans. by G. T. Thomson. New York: Harper and Row.

Biebuyck, D., and Mateene, K. C. (eds. and trans.)
   1969   *The Mwindo Epic: From the Banyanga.* Berkeley and Los Angeles: University of California Press.

Brown, Raymond E.
   1984   "The Author Replies." *Commonweal* 111 (Feb. 24): 100.

de Kerckhove, Derrick
   1985   "The Alphabet and the Brain." Paper presented at the International Colloquium on Innis, McLuhan and the Frontier of Communication, University of Toronto, March 8–9.

Farrell, Thomas J.
   1983   "IQ and Standard English." *College Composition and Communication* 34: 470–484.
   1984   "Gospel, Oral and Written." *Commonweal* 111 (Feb. 24): 100.

Fleming, David L.
    1969   *"Passion" in the Spiritual Writings of Teilhard de Chardin: A
              Study of Detachment and Diminishment*. Dissertation, The
              Catholic University of America, Washington, D.C.

Foley, John Miles
    1985   *Oral-Formulaic Theory and Research: An Introduction and An-
              notated Bibliography*. New York and London, ENG: Garland
              Publishing.

Frye, Northrop
    1982   *The Great Code: The Bible and Literature*. New York and
              London, ENG: Harcourt Brace Jovanovich.

Havelock, Eric A.
    1963   *Preface to Plato*. Cambridge, MA: Belknap Press of Harvard
              University Press.
    1978   *The Greek Concept of Justice: From Its Shadow in Homer to Its
              Substance in Plato*. Cambridge, MA and London, ENG: Har-
              vard University Press.
    1982   *The Literate Revolution in Greece and Its Cultural Con-
              sequences*. Princeton: Princeton University Press.

Heron, A. and Dowel, W.
    1974   "The Questionable Unity of the Concrete Operations Stage."
              International Journal of Psychology 9: 1–9.

Kelber, Werner H.
    1983   *The Oral and the Written Gospel: The Hermeneutics of Speaking
              and Writing in the Synoptic Tradition, Mark, Paul, and Q*.
              Philadelphia: Fortress Press.

Kellaghan, T.
    1968   "Abstraction and Categorization in African Children." *Interna-
              tional Journal of Psychology* 3: 115–120.

Lévi-Strauss, Claude
    1966   *The Savage Mind*. Chicago: The University of Chicago Press.

Lohr, Charles H.
    1961   "Oral Techniques in the Gospel of Matthew." *Catholic Biblical
              Quarterly* 23: 403–435.

Lord, Albert B.
    1960   *The Singer of Tales*. Cambridge, MA: Harvard University Press.

Luria, A. R.
    1976   *Cognitive Development: Its Cultural and Social Foundations*.
              Trans. by M. Lopez–Morillas and L. Solotaroff; ed. by M. Cole.
              Cambridge, MA and London, ENG: Harvard University Press.

Lynch, William F.
    1960   *Christ and Apollo: The Dimensions of the Literary Imagination*.
              New York: Sheed and Ward.

Maxwell, Kevin B.
  1983   *Bemba Myth and Ritual: The Impact of Literacy on an Oral Culture*. New York, Frankfurt on the Main, and Berne: Peter Lang.

McNamee, Maurice B.
  1960   *Honor and the Epic Hero: A Study of the Shifting Concept of Magnanimity in Philosophy and Epic Poetry*. New York: Holt, Rinehart, and Winston.

Notopoulos, James A.
  1949   "Parataxis in Homer." *Transactions of the American Philological Association* 80: 1–23.

Ong, Walter J.
  1958   *Ramus, Method, and the Decay of Dialogue: From the Art of Discourse to the Art of Reason*. Cambridge, MA: Harvard University Press.
  1967   *The Presence of the Word: Some Prolegomena for Cultural and Religious History*. New Haven and London, ENG: Yale University Press.
  1971   *Rhetoric, Romance, and Technology: Studies in the Interaction of Expression and Culture*. Ithaca, NY and London, ENG: Cornell University Press.
  1977   *Interfaces of the Word: Studies in the Evolution of Consciousness*. Ithaca, NY and London, ENG: Cornell University Press.
  1982a   *Orality and Literacy: The Technologizing of the Word*. London, ENG and New York: Methuen.
  1982b   "Introduction: On Saying We and Us to Literature." Pp. 3–7 in *Three American Literatures*. Ed. by Houston A. Baker, Jr. New York: The Modern Language Association of America.

Perry, Ben E.
  1937   "The Early Greek Capacity for Viewing Things Separately." *Transactions of the American Philological Association* 68: 403–27.

Schneidau, Herbert N.
  1977   *Sacred Discontent: The Bible and Western Tradition*. Berkeley, Los Angeles, and London, ENG: University of California Press.

Scribner, Sylvia and Cole, Michael
  1981   *The Psychology of Literacy*. Cambridge, MA and London, ENG: Harvard University Press.

van Beeck, Frans Jozef
  1983   "Reflections on a Dated Book." *The Heythrop Journal* 24: 51–57.

Zerwick, Maximilian
  1963   *Biblical Greek*. Trans. by Joseph Smith, S.J. Rome: Scripta Pontificii Instituti Biblici.

PETER'S DENIAL AS POLEMIC OR CONFESSION: THE IMPLICATIONS OF MEDIA CRITICISM FOR BIBLICAL HERMENEUTICS

Thomas E. Boomershine
United Theological Seminary

ABSTRACT

Werner Kelber's recent study of the history of the gospel tradition, *The Oral and the Written Gospel*, raises three interrelated questions that grow out of awareness of the role of the medium in the gospel tradition: the purpose of the characterization of Peter and the disciples in Mark's Gospel, the relationship between the oral and written forms of the gospel tradition in the first century, and the methodology of contemporary biblical criticism. Kelber's reconstruction of the relationship between the oral and the written gospel is based on an exegesis of the purpose of the characterization of Peter and the disciples in the Gospel of Mark. According to Kelber, Mark's purpose is to create alienation from Peter and the disciples and the oral gospel which they represent.

A recognition of the interdependence of the medium and the meaning of biblical texts raises a foundational issue. Methodologies based on silent reading of ancient texts create the potential for distortion in the perception and understanding of Biblical texts that were intended to be experienced as sound. A primary symptom of that potential distortion is increased psychological distance: i.e., the absence of sympathetic involvement. The evidence from the ancient world shows clearly that ancient authors including Mark assumed that their works would be read aloud. If Mark's material is experienced as an oral reading in a manner appropriate to the assumptions of ancient authors, Kelber's exegesis is improbable as a description of Mark's intention. This finding in turn raises major questions about Kelber's reconstruction of the relationship between the oral and the written gospel.

The clarification of the competing hermeneutical circles organized around oral and silent reading may help to shed light on the
role of the medium in which biblical texts are interpreted both in
the ancient and the modern context. Silent reading of biblical
texts is anachronistic. It is media eisegesis. In light of this analysis, those scholars who have implicitly argued for the centrality of
oral reading of the biblical texts have identified a central methodological issue.

0.   Werner Kelber's recent book, *The Oral and the Written Gospel*,
explores the implications of contemporary media research for the interpretation of the Gospel tradition. Recent investigations of existing oral
cultures (Lord, Finnegan) and the patterns associated with media transi-
tions (McLuhan, Ong) have shown that a change in the dominant mode of
communication within a culture, particularly the transition from oral
speech to writing, invariably involves a major transformation of communication styles, patterns of community organization, and ways of
thinking. In classical form criticism, the relationship between the oral
and the written Gospel was understood as a linear relationship of substantial continuity. Kelber argues that, in the light of this more recent
research, a more appropriate picture of the gospel tradition would
emphasize the chasm that separates the gospel in the world of writing
from the gospel in its original oral matrix. Kelber's central thesis, "that
the written gospel is ill accounted for, and in fact misunderstood, as the
sum total of oral rules and drives" (214), generates a radically new picture
of the history of the gospel tradition.
01.   A central component of Kelber's thesis is that Mark was carrying out
a polemic against Peter and the disciples as representatives of the oral
gospel. In his earlier works, especially *The Kingdom in Mark* (1974), Prof.
Kelber developed the now widely held position in Markan scholarship
that Mark portrayed the disciples and Peter in a highly negative light in
order to discredit them as representatives of a form of Jewish Christianity
centered in Jerusalem to which Mark was opposed (1974: 64, 146–7).
Kelber's argument here is an extension and further development of that
argument. In light of the chasm separating the media worlds of oral
speech and writing, Kelber sees Mark as criticizing the disciples and
particularly Peter as representatives of not only the Jerusalem church but
also of the entire tradition of the oral gospel (97, 130).
0.2   A formative analogy underlying Kelber's study is Eric Havelock's
conclusion in his *Preface to Plato* that Plato banished the poets (rhapsodes) from his republic as part of his polemic against the oral culture
formed around the recitation of Homeric poetry. Just as Plato attacked
the poets as representatives of the Homeric oral world and its educational
system, so also Mark disassociated the gospel from the disciples who

represented the heterodox world of the oral gospel (95–7, 194–5). As Kelber writes:

> Mark's writing is fueled with a passion to disown the voices of his oral precursors. One is struck by this gospel's repudiation of the disciples, the prophets, and the family of Jesus. In sociological terms, Mark undermines the very structures that facilitate and legitimize oral transmission: the legitimately appointed authorities, the charismatic authorities, and the hereditary authorities. The very representatives of Jesus, those who can and must be expected to function as official, inspired, and traditional transmitters of his words, are dislodged. The guarantors of the tradition have been evicted. (104)

Stated in terms of narrative analysis, Mark's project was intended to create maximum distance between the Jesus tradition and the oral gospel represented by Peter and the disciples.

0.3   Kelber's analysis constitutes a hermeneutical circle. His picture of Mark as operating on the other side of the chasm between the oral and the written gospel is based on the exegesis of Mark's characterization of Peter and the disciples. This exegesis is in turn generated by a redaction critical methodology in which the tradition is analyzed from a highly distanced perspective. This picture is thoroughly congruent with the primary orientation of contemporary biblical criticism and the media world within which it has operated. However, the very basis of Kelber's analysis, the impact of media change, raises questions about the methodological paradigm of contemporary historical criticism.

The Basis for Media Criticism

1.0   A major contribution of contemporary media research is to call attention to the distance that exists between the epistemological worlds of modern and ancient experience of texts. The results of recent research into the impact of media change have made it clear, as Father Ong and Prof. Kelber have shown so clearly in their work, that media changes constitute a revolution in consciousness. A differentiated treatment of texts that were intended for being heard and those intended for silent reading is a necessary implication of this recognition. Walter Ong has asked an important question:

> How far does the reading of the Bible today call for re-establishing the relationship between the text and the reader distinctive of the highly oral culture of the Biblical age, when

writing was far less interiorized in the psyche than it normally is
today in highly technologized cultures?

If the medium does significantly influence the meaning of a biblical
tradition, the answer to Ong's question is that historical interpretation
requires an effort to experience the tradition in its intended medium.
1.1   The reason for this necessity is clarified by Aristotle's analysis of the
causes of meaning in poetry. Aristotle identifies three causes of the
overall effect or meaning of poetry, the object, manner, and means of
poetic imitation. Thus, Aristotle's opening methodological paragraph:

> Now epic poetry, tragedy, comedy, dithyrambic poetry, and most
> forms of flute and lyre playing all happen to be, in general,
> imitations, but they differ from each other in three ways: either
> because the imitation is carried on by different means or because
> it is concerned with different kinds of objects or because it is
> present, not in the same, but in a different manner (5).

1.12   The object and manner of imitation are approximate correlates of
our understanding of form and content. The object of imitation refers to
the subject matter or characteristic content of different types of poetry:
e.g., tragedy imitates noble men and comedy baser types. In relation to
the manner of poetry, Aristotle's basic distinction is between narration
and dramatization (11). He further refines the distinctions between different forms of verse in the genres of tragedy, comedy, and epic (e.g., 19–
20).
1.13   The means or medium of imitation describes the materials from
which poetry is made. The medium of poetry is, first of all, sound.
Aristotle includes flute and lyre playing as a form of poetry in which there
is harmony and rhythm but no words. In dramatic narrative poetry,
therefore, language as spoken words is the medium. These spoken words
are further distinguished by the employment of rhythm, melody, or
harmony. The longer discussions of diction (Sections XX–XXII) and the
various meters of tragedy and epic (XXIII–XXIV) develop additional
aspects of the medium of poetry.
1.14   For Aristotle, these elements of poetry are causes which control
the over-all effect of poetry. This corresponds to Aristotle's understanding
of the causes which produce all phenomena, natural or artificial. The
relationship of the elements of poetry and the causes can be seen in the
following chart:

Cause	In Art Generally	In Poetry
Material:	Means or medium	Sound, language, rhythm, harmony
Formal:	Object or content	Actions with agents
Efficient:	Manner or form	Narrative, epic, dramatic

1.2   Contemporary media research has made clear the foundational accuracy of Aristotle's analysis. McLuhan's characteristically exaggerated statement of his basic conclusion is "the medium is the message"(7). While less comprehensive than Aristotle's more diversified analysis of the causal structure of poetry, McLuhan's phrase identifies an important fact: the medium has a determinative effect on the meaning. Media criticism is based on the recognition of the causal relationship between medium and meaning. Thus, Aristotle's analysis of the causes of the meaning of poetry and the particular development of Aristotle's insight in contemporary media criticism invites us to explore the original medium of the gospel tradition.

1.3   When applied to contemporary study of ancient texts, the implication of media criticism is that a change in the medium in which we study and experience an ancient text will inevitably change its meaning. Therefore, to the degree that our goal is to understand the meaning of the biblical documents in their original historical context, it is essential to know the medium in which they were intended to be experienced.

The Original Medium of Mark's Gospel

2.0   What was the intended medium of the oral and the written gospel? While Prof. Kelber acknowledges the evidence of oral reading in the ancient world (41–42, #193), the dominant description of Mark's textuality throughout the book is the silencing of the tradition. He writes, for example:

> Mark's writing project is an act of daring and rife with consequences. To the extent that the gospel draws on oral voices, it has rendered them voiceless. The voiceprints of once-spoken words have been muted. . . . For the moment, language has fallen silent.(91)

Kelber's analysis is in direct continuity with the basic assumption of form criticism that the writing of the tradition constitutes a more or less immediate transition to the media world of silent reading. This is a crucial assumption because it determines the modern critics' medium of perceiving the narrative. That is, Kelber assumes a more or less immediate transition from the medium of orality to the modern world of textual experience as silent reading.

2.1   This assumption is not unusual. Contemporary biblical scholarship has consistently assumed that the relationship of the original audience of the biblical literature was a relationship of readers to texts. Discussions about "the reader" and "the text" abound in 20th century historical critical exegesis. While there are often some qualifications of this paradigm with phrases such as "readers or hearers" and "audience," the general assumption is that biblical books such as the Gospel of Mark were read as documents by a single reader who read the document in silence. Thus, literary criticism of biblical texts has uncritically appropriated the paradigms of works such as Wolfgang Iser's *The Implied Reader* with the apparent assumption that a modern and an ancient reader's relationship to the text is the same.[1] The question is then: what did Mark assume about the manner in which his written Gospel would be experienced? Did Mark write a text that he assumed would be read in public or in private, aloud or in silence?

2.2   The evidence from the ancient world in regard to this issue is unambiguous. Manuscripts in the ancient world were virtually always read aloud. An ancient writer composed a text with the assumption that the text would be read aloud. Throughout most of ancient history, the readings were public readings. As Moses Hadas has summarized:

> Among the Greeks the regular method of publication was by public recitation, at first, significantly, by the author himself, and then by professional readers or actors, and public recitation continued to be the regular method of publication even after books and the art of reading had become common. (50)

From the rhapsodes who presented public recitations of heroic poetry to the performances of lyric and dramatic poetry by poets and actors, the ancient world was full of recitations of memorized texts in large public gatherings.

2.21   But even private readings were normally done aloud. Thus, St. Augustine (Confessions 5.3) describes his surprise at Ambrose's habit of silent reading: "while reading, his eyes glanced over the pages, and his heart searched out the sense, but his voice and tongue were silent." It was so unusual that visitors actually came to watch. Augustine goes on to explain this strange behavior of his revered mentor and suggests that concentration or preservation of his voice might have been motives, and concludes: "But whatever was his motive in so doing, doubtless in such a man was a good one." Further evidence of the association of silent reading with disrepute is evident in Lucian's satire of an ancient dabbler in books (*Adversus Indoctum* 2):

> What do all your books profit you, who are too ignorant to appreciate their value and beauty? To be sure you look upon them with open eyes and even greedily, and some of them you read at a great pace, *your eye outstripping your voice;* but I do not consider that sufficient, unless you know the merits and defects of all that is written there, and understand what every sentence means.

Thus, Lucian assumed that understanding the full meaning required reading aloud. This reflects the assumption of the ancient world that any learned man would read aloud even when reading privately.

2.22   The evidence in regard to reading aloud in the ancient world is readily available and has been for some time. In 1926, Josef Balogh published two long articles entitled "Voces Paginarum" in which he collected references in classical literature to the oral reading of manuscripts. And in his book, *Ancilla to Classical Reading*, Moses Hadas both cites most of this evidence and discusses it in a highly accessible and entertaining manner. Another major source of evidence regarding the prevalence of the oral reading of manuscripts is the history of annotation. From the trope marks of the Masoretic text to the marginal notes in Greek texts, ancient authors and editors developed systems of annotation in order to provide guidance for readers about how to read the text aloud rightly.[2]

2.23   In the Biblical tradition, the oral reading of manuscripts is reflected in many places. A short list of major public and private readings in the Biblical tradition is indicative of the tradition:

> 1) The discovery and reading of the Deuteronomy scroll (II Kings 22): "And the King went up to the house of the Lord and with him all the men of Judah and all the inhabitants of Jerusalem, and the priests and the prophets, all the people, both small and great, and he read in their hearing all the words of the book of the covenant which had been found in the house of the Lord."
>
> 2) The reading of the scroll of the prophecies of Jeremiah (Jeremiah 36): Baruch read the scroll of Jeremiah's prophecies aloud at the Temple gate and it was reported to the king. The King then ordered the scroll read aloud to him as he sat on the winter porch. As it was read, he cut up the scroll and fed it into a brazier.
>
> 3) The covenant renewal festival after the exile (Nehemiah 8): Ezra read the Torah all day long before the people of Israel at the Water Gate while the Levites provided oral interpretation of the reading as Ezra read.
>
> 4) The conversion of the Ethiopian eunuch (Acts 8): Phillip heard the Ethiopian eunuch reading the prophet Isaiah aloud in his chariot and interpreted the text orally in relation to Jesus.
>
> 5) The instructions for the reading of the Revelation of John (Revelation 1:2): "Blessed is he who reads aloud the words of the prophecy, and blessed are those who hear, and who keep what is written therein; for the time is near."

2.24   There is, as far as I can discover, no evidence of silent reading in the Biblical tradition. Studies of the words relating to reading in both Hebrew and Greek yield no signs of anything that might be construed as silent reading.

2.25   Therefore, the answer to the question of Mark's intended medium is that Mark would have assumed that his Gospel would be read aloud, either from a manuscript or from memory, probably in a public reading. The only other option in the media world of Mark's day was a private oral reading. And that would have required the unlikely assumption of extensive copying and distribution of Mark's manuscript. Silent reading was, if it existed in the first century, an extraordinary and disrespected idiosyncrasy. Private reading aloud was more frequent but, because of the scarceness of texts, remained a luxury available to relatively few individuals.

2.3   The irony of the current state of biblical studies is that the recognition of public reading as the intended medium of ancient literature has been known for decades. It has become virtually a commonplace in the study of medieval literature. But in the study of much earlier biblical literature, this recognition has received little or no attention.

2.4   In the light of the recognition of the medium as a primary cause of the meaning of texts, the implications of the prevalence of reading aloud in the ancient world for historical biblical criticism are significant. To the degree that our goal is to understand the meaning of the biblical texts in their original historical context, we need to study and experience the texts in their original medium, namely, as sounds recited and heard at least in private but preferably in public readings.

2.41   An analogy from music may be helpful. The symphonies and operas of Mozart, for example, were originally composed to be heard. The original medium was sound. But Mozart's compositions were printed and can now be studied as documents. Our present pattern of experiencing biblical traditions is as if we were primarily to study Mozart's scores and talk about them without ever performing or listening to his music. Just as experiencing the impact of Mozart's *Requiem* or *The Magic Flute* by only reading the score would be very difficult for most of us, so also to primarily study the texts of the biblical traditions without reciting and hearing them is to limit our experience of the traditions to a secondary and derivative medium.

2.5   If the understanding and reestablishment of the original medium is a desirable component in the methodology of contemporary biblical study, how would we do it? One step in that direction is to test interpretations by public readings. This is one way in which we can begin to experience the biblical material in its intended medium. Therefore, I propose that we use the test of oral interpretation in evaluating the alternative interpretations of Peter's denial.

2.51   However, it is difficult to demonstrate different oral interpretations in writing. And *Semeia* does not have the technical capabilities to send along audio tapes. Therefore, I would ask that you, as the reader, do the testing yourself. I will suggest ways of reading the text aloud, a kind of modern annotation. You can then test the interpretations orally by reading tham aloud to yourself. Admittedly this is only a private rather than a public reading. And later an even more valid test would be to read the story aloud to a group. But we have to start somewhere. And, in this way, we can at least take a small step toward testing interpretations in the Gospel's intended medium.

Mark's Characterization of Peter

3.0   The general structure of the evidence for the interpretation of Mark's emphasis on the failure of the disciples and Peter as a critique of the theological position they represent is well known.[3] In this reading of Mark, the negative elements in the characterization of the disciples are understood as connected with an effort to discredit the disciples and all that they represent.

3.1   For the purposes of this methodological test, the story of Peter's denial is an excellent focus. In Kelber's reading of the Markan tradition, the story of Peter's denial is the culmination of Mark's effort throughout the Gospel to discredit Peter and the disciples. I quote:

> If the hopes of the gospel's recipients (that the disciples will faithfully follow) have been kept alive into the passion story, it is there that they are decisively crushed. Far from experiencing a change of heart, the disciples, under the leadership of Peter, play out their roles of outsiders to the bitter end. Peter contradicts Jesus' prediction of the discipleship failure (14.26–29), all the disciples promise to suffer with Jesus (14.30–31), the triumvirate falters at Gethsemane at the moment of arrest (14.50), and Peter, the last hope denies Jesus while the latter makes his fateful confession before the high priest (14.53–72) (128).

Stated in terms of narrative analysis, Mark's characterization of Peter is a polemical characterization in which the positive hopes and expectations of the gospel's audience for Peter and the disciples are all broken. The purpose of this characterization is to alienate the audience from Peter and the theology he represents.

3.11   The structure of a polemical characterization is relatively easy to identify. First, the norms of judgment that operate in the characterization are negative. The narrator appeals for the audience to recognize that the character's actions are wrong. Second, the dynamics of distance create an intensification of alienation and there is an appeal to the audience for total separation from and opposition to the character.

3.12   According to Kelber, this is what happens in the characterization of Peter, the disciples, and the women at the end of the Gospel. Clearly the sleeping, flight, and denial of the disciples and Peter are wrong. The norms of judgment are absolutely clear. And in the characterization of Peter, Mark seeks to create maximum alienation from the disciples and

Peter as a way of discrediting them and the oral Gospel that they represent.

3.13   If this was Mark's intention, the implications for the appropriate oral reading of Mark's text are relatively easy to identify. If Mark had annotated his manuscript with instructions for oral recitation, he would have instructed the reader to condemn Peter for his failure. The story would be read in a spirit of judgment and make a strong appeal for alienation from Peter. In effect, the reciter would point his finger at Peter and condemn him for his failure and thereby appeal to the listeners to join him in opposition to Peter. A tone of mockery or ridicule might be an additional element in an appropriate oral rendering.

3.14   I would suggest that you try this interpretation by reading the story of Peter's denial aloud. The goal of this reading is to evaluate the interpretation in its intended medium. Throughout the reading, point your finger at Peter and, at the end of the story, condemn or mock him as he realizes his guilt. Thus, the end of the story was a highly cynical satire and a bitter polemic. The so-called father of the church was really a coward and a misguided leader who never understood who Jesus was.

3.15   As I have sought to recite the story, this oral interpretation has seemed unsatisfactory. It inevitably comes off as somewhat moralistic and has the feel of a childish taunt. The oral reading reveals an anomaly. Clearly, Peter's denial is wrong as is the sleeping of the three and the flight of the disciples. But the impact of the story is not polemical. It is a historical fact that people have not been alienated from Peter when they have heard the story of his denial over the centuries. The story has not had that effect. If anything, people have loved and revered Peter, particularly in relation to this story. Why?

3.2   I would propose that the reason is a consistent pattern in the characterization of Peter.[4] There are three places in Mark's characterization of Peter in which Peter's actions are associated with negative norms of judgment: 1) Peter's rebuke in response to Jesus' first passion prophecy to which Jesus responds, "Get behind me, Satan" (8.31–33); 2) Gethsemane in which Peter falls asleep and is rebuked by Jesus (14.36–41); 3) the denial. There is absolutely no ambiguity about the norms involved in these actions. Mark clearly appeals for his listeners to recognize that each of these actions of Peter is wrong.

3.21   But Mark does not appeal for alienation from Peter. Stated in terms of dynamics of distance, the characterization of an enemy is structurally consistent. The classic pattern of the Western is as indicative as the characterization of Pharaoh, Goliath, or the chief priests. There is a steady intensification of appeals for alienation from the character so that the distance relationship to the character steadily grows. In the classic western just as in the story of David and Goliath, the bad guy is an alien threat at the beginning who gradually does things that are worse and worse until the audience cheers when he is killed by the good guy.

3.22   The characterization of Peter does not fit this pattern. He does some things that are, according to the narrative's norms of judgment, clearly wrong. But, after each instance of wrongdoing, Mark takes explicit steps to reestablish a sympathetic relationship with Peter. The clearest element in this narrative structure is a sympathetic inside view in which Peter's feelings are described. Recognition of this pattern in the characterization will help to identify another possible intention in Mark's telling of Peter's denial.

3.3   The fight between Jesus and Peter over Jesus' passion prophecy is immediately preceded by Peter's confession of Jesus as Messiah. In terms of the norms of the narrative, Peter is the first character in the story to recognize what the narrator announced in the first sentence, namely, Jesus is the Christ. It is a very positive norm and creates a high degree of positive feeling in relation to Peter. After the fight, Mark reestablishes this sympathic relationship with Peter in the transfiguration narrative. Jesus is transfigured, Moses and Elijah appear, and the three of them are talking. Peter's offer to build three booths for them is followed by a narrative comment: "For he did not know what to say. For they were afraid."

3.31   These narrative comments beginning with *gar* are typical of Mark's use of this form. They are consistently used to explain a puzzle or surprise that has been created for his audience by the previous statement (e.g., 1:16, 22; 2:15; 3:21; 5:8, 28, 42; 6:17, 18, 20, 31, 48; 9:34; 10:22; 11:13; 14:2, 40 56; 15:10; 16:4, 8). In this instance, these comments apparently explain why Peter was so nervous and why he said such an inept and inappropriate thing. The explanation is thoroughly sympathetic and is clearly an appeal for identification with Peter whose feelings are presented as the way any person would feel in such company. In the technical terms of narrative analysis, this is a narrative comment to the audience which gives an inside view into Peter's internal thoughts and feelings. And the norms of judgment are wholly sympathetic and humanly understandable.[5]

3.32   The best way to understand the dynamics of a story like this is to hear another story that has similar characteristics. What follows is my effort to identify such a story. But, in order for it to be appropriate in the context of this scholarly discussion, you need to imagine this story being told in a somewhat folksy style among a group of friends.

3.33   Peter's response to being in the presence of Jesus, Moses, and Elijah is like a mythical Midwestern B.D. student of Paul Tillich's at Union in the early '60s finding himself unexpectedly thrust into the midst of a private conversation at a seminary tea between Bultmann, Barth, and Tillich. And Mark describes his bumbling effort to figure out something to say. To pursue my analogy, with which every present or former graduate student should be able to identify—"It's a good thing I'm here, Paul. Could I get some coffee for you and Karl and Rudolf?" Why would he say such a stupid thing? Because he didn't know what to say. For he was afraid. It is Biblical humor at its best and Peter is the one with whom we can all identify in that spot.

3.4   The Gethesemane story has a similar structure. Peter's falling asleep is preceded by Jesus inviting his three closest friends to be with him in his hour of need. When Peter falls asleep, Jesus rebukes him. But, in the next episode, when Jesus again finds them sleeping, Mark once again inserts a narrative comment in which he interrupts the action to give an inside view into the disciples' situation: "For their eyes were weighed down. And they didn't know what to say to him."

3.41   The first narrative comment explains the surprise of their going to sleep a second time by describing the external power which they could not control. Once again, it is thoroughly sympathetic. The requirements for wine consumption at Passover meals were probably known to most of Mark's audience. The expectations only *begin* with the required five cups of wine during a three to four hour feast. I observe that many people are like myself for whom two cups of wine will generally put them to sleep within thirty minutes after a big meal. Mark's appeal to his audience is to understand why the disciples' eyes were weighed down as they sat under a tree after the Passover meal while their teacher prayed long into the night.

3.42   The second comment is equally sympathetic in its appeal. The internal description of their inability to find something to say concretizes their shame. What does one say when a beloved friend has been disappointed in his greatest hour of need, even if it couldn't be helped? These narrative comments are inside views explaining their situation and their feelings. The comments do not in any way indicate that the disciples' going to sleep was anything other than wrong. But the narrative function of these comments is to enable the listeners to understand and sympathize with their inability to stay awake. Thus, the episode is an appeal for sympathetic identification and prevents alienation or negative distance.

3.5   Finally, and most graphically, this narrative structure is evident in the story of Peter's denial. Peter's three denials are reported one after another so that the audience can count them. The last denial is a climactic, highly emotional, and explicit denial of any relationship with Jesus. But, after the description of the cock crow, Mark concludes the story with the most extensive and poignant inside view in his entire narrative. He invites the audience literally to enter Peter's mind as he remembers, somewhat inaccurately, Jesus' prophecy. And the climax of the story is an invitation to witness and share Peter's grief.

3.51   This interpretation can now be tested by oral reading. The episodes describing the first two denials are to be read dispassionately except for the words of both the maid and Peter. The climax of Peter's third denial should be read with extremely high emotional intensity and volume. The ending of the story, beginning with "And Peter remembered," is an intimate description of what was going on in Peter's mind. The usual translation of the ambiguous word, *epibalon,* is "breaking down." A better translation is "beating on himself" and describes the gesture of striking the chest which the storyteller may have used in this last sentence. The goal of the reading of these words is to express Peter's realization of his failure and his grief as deeply and graphically as possible.

3.6   What is the difference in these two interpretations? It is the difference between a pointed finger and a clutched fist beating oneself in grief, between an ideological judgment and the expression of a deeply internalized recognition of a monumental wrong. The options for the interpretation are that Mark's intention was either to invite his audience to share in criticizing Peter for his failure or to share in the grief of Peter's own realization of his failure. It is either an anti-Petrine polemic or a Petrine confession.

3.7   What difference does oral reading make in deciding between these two options? Could not the same conclusions be drawn from an analysis of the narrative characteristics of the Markan text without any oral experience? As Robert Tannehill's article on the disciples in Mark (1977) demonstrates, it is certainly possible for an analysis of Mark's narrative as a silent text to lead to the same conclusion that Mark's intention in the characterization of Peter and the disciples was not theological polemic.

3.71   The question is whether the polemical reading is more historically probable as a description of the intended meaning of Mark's narrative in its original context. It is in relation to this question that the medium makes a difference. When the narrative is read aloud in a manner as close as possible to the patterns of oral recitation implicit in the narrative, the anti-Petrine interpretation is much less probable. The reason is the difference in psychological distance to the text and, in this story, to Peter that is required for oral recitation in contrast to silent reading.

3.72   When the text is studied in silence, the degree of potential distance in relation to the text and to Peter is greater. It is possible to stand apart from the narrative event and to evaluate Peter and his actions with a high degree of dispassionate objectivity. Silent readers *can* imaginatively enter into the dynamics of the story as an oral narrative, in part by recreating the sounds of the story in their minds. There is nothing in silent reading that makes impossible a higher degree of sympathetic distance in relation to Mark's story of Peter's denial. But it is only a possibility. In the modern age, when psychological distance from texts has increased, reading aloud rather than in silence makes certain interpretations of Peter's denial improbable because it requires a higher degree of sympathetic participation in the story.

3.8 I have found Prof. Kelber's delineation of the theological issues implicit in these disagreements illuminating and exegetically accurate. I agree that Mark is opposed to a simple *theios aner* Christology. That issue is implicit in the conflicts with Peter and the disciples. But how is that issue worked out in the story? Prof. Kelber has rightly identified the theological ideas that influenced Mark's work as a shaper of the gospel tradition. But he misunderstands the nature of Mark's craft and the medium for which he wrote his stories. Indeed, given the centrality of Kelber's interpretation of disciple failure to his thesis, this misunderstanding raises serious questions about the over-all picture of the oral and written Gospel that he has drawn.

The Oral and the Written Gospel

4.0 In my judgment, Werner Kelber has established a new set of questions for historical criticism and has proposed a series of hypotheses that require careful evaluation and further research. Kelber's hypothesis that Mark was involved in an anti-Petrine polemic is historically improbable. While Kelber has demonstrated that the documents can be understood in this way, the question is whether the reading is historically probable. The narrative structure of Peter's characterization and the study of the narrative in its intended medium show that it is unlikely that the story had this meaning in its original historical context.

4.1 My evaluation is that Kelber has collapsed 1900 years of media development into a forty year period in the first century. The degree of psychological distance from the Markan text that is required in order to even conceive the hypothesis that Mark was engaged in a polemic against Peter has only happened since the 18th century. The process of increasing distance and alienation from the word as sound has taken nineteen centuries, not forty years.

4.11 Furthermore, is it likely that a movement as weak and vulnerable as the Christian sect in the post A.D. 70 period would produce and later canonize a first gospel that was a polemic against its primary and most highly respected leaders? Movements that are divided to this degree rarely survive and grow because the competing leaders cancel each other out.

4.12 I doubt that this story would have become a cornerstone of the tradition unless Peter told it and permitted it to be told about him. The same was true of Paul. He told the story of his persecution of the church. In the context of the importance that people in the ancient world attached to how they were remembered, these stories are striking. What is the spirit of men who would tell such stories about themselves? They are the stories of men who have experienced the forgiveness and power of God to overcome their weaknesses and failures. How does one tell such a story? One tells such a story as a confession and as an invitation to others who have the same feelings to identify with the story and make it their own.

4.2   Such a conclusion raises serious questions about other aspects of Prof. Kelber's synthesis. If a Markan polemic against Peter and the disciples is historically improbable, so also is a polemic against the oral gospel. Does this imply that Kelber's emphasis on the chasm between the oral and the written gospel is also inaccurate? Kelber has established that the transition from orality to writing was a major development in the gospel tradition. The question is whether Kelber has accurately described the character of that transition. The character of reading in the ancient world and the analysis of the narrative structure of Peter's denial leads to the conclusion that the degree of separation and psychological distance from the living oral word that Kelber finds in Mark only happened later. We need, therefore, to identify the bridges across the chasm between the oral and the written gospel.

4.21   The phenomenology of sound in the first century is one of those bridges. The gospel continued to be read aloud. The transition from the oral to the written gospel in Mark's context was not a transition from sound to silence but from sounds recomposed by a storyteller to sounds read from a manuscript. We need to know more about the character of the sounds of the gospel narratives in the oral and the written gospel.

4.22   A second bridge is memory. The gospel narratives also continued to be told from memory. The transition to the written gospel did not mean the end of memorization and internalization of the tradition. A primary educational practice of the ancient world was the memorization of traditions written down in manuscripts. Thus, while the character of memorization changed as the gospel was written down, it was not eliminated.[6]

4.23   Indeed, the phenomenon of the memorization of manuscripts in the ancient world as a transitional stage between orality and literacy may have major implications for the Synoptic problem. The basic change between the memorization of oral traditions and the memorization of manuscripts is the much higher degree of word for word memory in manuscript memorization.[7] However, the memorization and recomposition of manuscripts is an entirely different process from the editing of documents. Thus, the possibility exists that Matthew and Luke may have memorized Mark and then recomposed his gospel preserving both Mark's order and many of the stories virtually word for word. This combination—the discipline to reduplicate the tradition word for word and the freedom to reshape the tradition—may be a more accurate understanding of the process of the Synoptic tradition than the traditional model of the editing of documents. Such a model is also radically different from Herder's "oral Gospel" proposal with which Kelber has so generously associated me (1983:78).

4.3 The improbability of an anti-Petrine polemic in Mark raises further questions about the appropriateness of the analogy of Plato's polemic against the poets. The analogy breaks down in significant ways. Mark was not a Plato who developed philosophical and conceptual thought and who wrote dialogues and allegories. Mark continued like the poets to tell the stories. And the Church did not disassociate itself from the storytellers and poets of the traditions of Israel in the way that Plato disassociated the Academy from the rhapsodes and the Homeric traditions. Indeed, the Church canonized their writings and revered Peter as the first Pope. The formation of theology as the dominant mode of thought in early Christianity is analogous to Plato's development of philosophy and Mark stands at the beginning of that process. But Mark's role in the process of media transition of a first century Jewish sect is radically different from that of Plato in Athens.

4.31 Furthermore, while accepting the Platonic analogy, Kelber has rejected the oral tradition analogy with equal force. One of the ironies of Kelber's study is the degree to which he has ignored the results of oral tradition research since the development of form criticism. While it is true that there are distinctive ways in which oral traditions are ordered in the transition to writing, the implication of Kelber's study is that the entire process of ordering is foreign to oral tradition. His picture of the oral gospel is similar to the picture of classical form criticism of a series of individual short stories that were told independently and, apparently, one at a time.

4.32 The evidence from oral tradition research does not support this conclusion. The major field studies of oral traditions in recent years share a common conclusion that storytelling occasions are frequently long. They are certainly not two or three minute occasions of storytelling.[8] The stories may be ordered in different ways on different occasions. But the stories are lined up and told in a sequence that often goes on for hours. Thus, the historical probabilities are high that the pre-Markan storytellers told a *long* series of stories about Jesus and ordered them in different ways for different occasions.

4.34 However, while I suspect that there were long stories of Jesus' life, passion, death and resurrection told prior to Mark, I also find it historically probable that Mark brought a new degree of order and completeness to the tale when he wrote it down. And there may well have been in Mark's written gospel a new level of concentration on the ideas implicit in the story. Nevertheless, the evaluation of the exegetical foundation for Kelber's synthesis through media testing raises serious questions and reservations about the over-all picture of Mark that Kelber has drawn. These are then some of the questions upon which further research is needed in the aftermath of Kelber's study.

The Methodology of Historical Criticism

5.0   The most far-reaching problem that awareness of the role of the medium in biblical interpretation poses for contemporary criticism is the awareness of the chasm that separates the media world of historical criticism from the media world of the Bible. What are the methodological implications of the ancient assumption of reading aloud?

5.1   What is at stake here is the impact of media research on the way in which we study and interpret the Bible. In my view, we need to recognize the vast distance that separates our media world from the media world of the communities that developed the Bible. The greatest difference is that they were far closer to an oral world and its ways of thought than are we. Prof. Kelber's study tends to minimize that distance by reading back into the ancient world and specifically into the interpretation of Mark the characteristic relationships to texts of modern historical criticism.

5.11   The recognition of the role of the medium in contemporary Biblical scholarship may shed light on the long stream of reaction against the documentary hypothesis on the part of Jewish scholars.[9] One of the differences between Jewish and Christian scholarship on the Pentateuch is the medium in which Jewish scholars have experienced the Biblical literature. Jewish scholars have continued to hear the Pentateuch read aloud during each liturgical year. Christian scholars, on the other hand, have primarily studied the texts as silent documents. Many of the differences in the assessment of phenomena such as frequent parallelism in the Pentateuchal tradition may be related to this radical difference in the medium in which it is experienced.

5.12   A fascinating instance reflecting this difference in the study of the Gospel tradition can be seen in Lou Silberman's lecture for the Trinity University Colloquy on the Relationships of the Gospels in 1977. Silberman's lecture explores "wandering motifs" in the various literatures of Judaism of the Hellenistic era and the ways in which those motifs are interpreted. His final section is entitled, "Conclusion: How to Hear a Text." He argues that the assumption of literary sources in contemporary biblical study reflects the degree to which we "still march along the straight black line of the Gutenberg galaxy." He finds that the treatment of these themes by the various storytellers is different from the literary models of redaction. By the simple juxtaposition of traditional materials, the storytellers have brought to light latent possibilities of meaning in the stories. This latent meaning is directly related to hearing:

'Redactor' thus understood is one who senses the *latent* possibilities within a tradition and, by his placing of the tradition in a
particular context, manifests *a* possibility that may obscure but
not efface others. To hearers at home in a tradition, it is the
tensions between manifestation and latency that enriches and
enlarges the meaning of the story (217).

As an illustration he describes the chanting of the Book of Esther which I
will quote at length:

In the synagogue, the Book of Esther is read traditionally at a
rather rapid rate with its own distinctive cantillation. Five verses,
however, are chanted more slowly and with the chant reserved for
the Book of Lamentations. The verses are: 1:7: "And they gave
them to drink in vessels of gold . . ."; 2:6: "who had been carried
away from Jerusalem with the captives that had been carried away
with Jeconiah king of Judah, whom Nebuchadnezzar the king of
Babylon had carried away"; 3:15: "but the city of Shushan was
thrown into confusion"; 4:16, which concludes with the words
"and if I perish, I perish"; and finally 8:6, whose opening words
ky 'ykkh "how can I" echo the opening word of Lamentations,
chapters 1,2, and 4, *'ykh*. The reason for this anomaly is evident
for several of the verses, but to understand its presence, in the
first, one must known that, according to a *haggadah*, the vessels
used by the king and his courtiers were none other than the
sacred vessels of the Temple of Jerusalem. (217)

In these instances, therefore, it is only in the hearing of the tradition that
the meaning can be perceived in its fullness. And it is only in the
appreciation and experience of the art of the storyteller that the Gospels
and the history of the gospel tradition can be appropriately understood.
Silberman thus appeals for approaching the Synoptic problem as hearers
and storytellers rather than as silent readers and critics.

5.13   However, in the responses no one dealt with the methodological
issue implicit in Silberman's argument. Both Sanders' response and the
seminar which followed discussed the issues only in terms of the first
century context. There was no recognition of the way in which this
methodological decision about the medium of scholarly investigation
predetermines our perception of the first century.

5.2   I perceive here two competing paradigms for which the line of
division has not been clearly defined. The paradigms are defined by the
medium of experiencing the texts: oral reading, in public gatherings as
well as privately, or the silent reading of documents. Those who read the
texts aloud as their methodology appeal to silent readers on the basis of
historical evidence of orality and its characteristics. But that is only a
secondary and derivative outcome of an earlier decision. Each group

appeals to the other about different sets of empirical evidence. Implicit in Lou Silberman's lecture is an appeal to approach the Synoptic problem through listening rather than looking for a solution, through an assessment of auditory rather than visual sense data. The same discrepancy is also present between Werner Kelber and myself. But those who read the texts aloud and those who read in silence will inevitably pass like ships in the night because they are discussing two different epistemological worlds.

5.21   Reflection on the role of the medium in biblical interpretation suggests that there is a reciprocal relationship between our conception of the way in which the texts were originally experienced and the way in which we study them now. Stated in methodological terms, the decision before contemporary biblical criticism is whether oral interpretation is an essential step, and perhaps even a goal, of the interpretive process. In both the study of the Pentateuch and the Gospels, the options are to continue to study the documents in silence or to read them aloud. In fact, awareness of the determinative role of the medium in the experienced meaning of texts implies that, as long as the decision continues to be made that silent reading is the normative medium for interpretation, the decisions about the outcome of the most foundational issues of interpretation have already been made. Non-literary options for understanding the history of the tradition have already been excluded from the possibility of meaningfulness.

5.2   Beneath the discussions about oral and documentary tradition histories lies an unidentified methodoligical issue: to read aloud or to read in silence. To the degree that our intention is to understand the meaning of the texts in their original context, those who have argued that listening to the texts is essential have virtually all of the historical evidence on their side. Silent reading of biblical texts is an anachronism, a reading back of contemporary reading conventions into the ancient world. It is media eisegesis.

5.23   Thus, it would be possible to divide modern scholarship into those who read aloud and those who read in silence. The question posed by Werner Kelber's study and by the history of Synoptic criticism is whether it is possible to reconstruct the history of the gospel tradition accurately if we experience that history in an alien and unintended medium. Can we rightly perceive that tradition and assess the role of telling, reading aloud, remembering, and hearing stories if we continue to study that tradition in our studies alone and in silence?

5.3   Both Kelber and I agree that media research is of great importance for Biblical exegesis and hermeneutics. But the importance that we find there is radically different. This difference argues that we need to continue the work on media criticism that Herder, Gunkel, Bultmann, Dibelius, Marxsen, Ong, and Kelber have begun. Kelber's proposed reinterpretation of the Synoptic tradition demonstrates that a critical assessment of the medium of the Gospel is as important to its understanding as criticism of its form and content. Whereas form criticism subsumed the medium of biblical tradition under the category of form, careful attention is needed to clarify the role of the medium both in the original formation of the Gospel and in the ongoing process of its interpretation.

NOTES

[1] The contemporary paradigm of the audience of Biblical traditions as a "reader" who reads texts alone in silence is clearly reflected in a recent issue of *Semeia* entitled "Reader Response Approaches to Biblical and Secular Texts." Robert Fowler's introductory essay, "Who is 'The Reader'?" is an excellent survey of recent developments in this area. Literary critics of Mark such as Robert Tannehill (1977) and Robert Fowler (1981) have appropriated the basic models of reader/text interaction as developed in the work of Wolfgang Iser (1974; 1978).

[2] Rutherford's study (1905) of annotation as a textual means for the guidance of oral readings in the ancient world is still an excellent introductory survey. The literature of music history (e.g., Werner, 1959, 1984) tracing the development of notations for cantillation of Hebrew, Greek and Latin Biblical texts is a primary source for detailed reconstruction of how the texts actually sounded.

[3] For a comprehensive bibliographical survey of the literature exploring Mark's portrayal of the disciples as a motif of theological polemic, see Werner Kelber, *The Oral and the Written Gospel* (1983), p. 132.

[4] Tannehill emphasizes that the polemical interpretation of the characterization of the disciples cannot explain its positive aspects. The pattern is an appeal for identification with the disciples by their positive evaluation in the early parts of the Gospel followed by the questioning that arises out of the disciples' inadequacy (1977: 395).

[5] For further discussion of the role of inside views and narrative comments in the Gospel of Mark, see Thomas E. Boomershine and Gilbert L. Bartholomew, "The Narrative Technique of Mark 16:8" in *JBL* 100 (1981), pp. 214–219.

[6] An unfortunate aspect of Morton Smith's devastating and appropriate critique of Gerhardsson's *Memory and Manuscript* [*JBL* 82 (1963), pp. 169–76] has been the degree to which the constructive elements of his work have been ignored. While Smith rightly argued that there is no evidence prior to 70 CE of word for word memorization in the pedagogical practice of either tha rabbis or Jesus, this does not mean, nor did Smith argue, that pre-70 students did not memorize at all. Gerhardsson's work documented the centrality of memorization in the educational techniques of teachers throughout the Hellenistic era. The differences between the pre-70 and post-70 periods of Judaism are with the types of memorization rather than with its presence or absence.

[7] Albert Lord observes that once the Yugoslavian songs he studied were memorized from a written manuscript the process of the oral tradition irrevocably changed: "The set, 'correct' text had arrived, and the death knell of the oral process had been sounded" (137). The memorizers were reproducers rather than recreators of the songs. While Lord bemoans this process in the Yugoslavian oral tradition, it may be that the Synoptic tradition represents an intermediate stage in which the traditional oral freedom to recompose and reorder the tradition was combined with the more detailed word for word reproduction of memorized manuscripts.

[8] The widely divergent studies of oral prose traditions in Crowley's work on storytelling in the Bahamas, Degh in Hungary, and Finnegan and Scheub in Africa all include descriptions of typical storytelling occasions in which stories are told for hours.

⁹For example, the commentaries of E. Cassuto have steadily called attention to the unifying oral elements in the Pentateuchal narratives over against the fracturing tendencies of critics in pursuit of disparate documents. Jewish exegesis in general has maintained a much closer relationship to the original medium of the tradition.

WORKS CONSULTED

Aristotle
  1953   *The Poetics*. Cambridge, Mass.: Harvard University Press.

Balogh, Josef
  1927   "Voces Paginarum: Beiträge zur Geschichte des lauten Lesens und Schreibens." *Philologus* 82: 84–109; 202–240.

Boomershine, Thomas E.
and Bartholomew, Gilbert L.
  1981   "The Narrative Technique of Mark 16:8." *Journal of Biblical Literature* 100: 213–223.

Crowley, Daniel J.
  1966   *I Could Talk Old-Story Good: Creativity in Bahamian Folklore*. University of California.

Degh, Linda
  1965   *Folktales of Hungary*. Trans. by Judit Halasz. *Folktales of the World*, ed. Richard M. Dorson. Chicago: University of Chicago Press.

Finnegan, Ruth
  1967   *Limba Stories and Story-Telling*. Oxford Library of African Literature. Oxford: Clarendon Press.
  1977   *Oral Poetry*. Cambridge: Cambridge University Press.

Fowler, Robert M.
  1985   "Who Is "the Reader" in Reader Response Criticism?" *Semeia* 31: 5–26.

Gerhardsson, Birger
  1961   *Memory and Manuscript*. Lund: C. W. K. Gleerup; Copenhagen: Ejnar Munksgaard.

Hadas, Moses
  1954   *Ancilla to Classical Reading*. New York: Columbia University Press.

Havelock, Eric
  1963   *Preface to Plato*. Cambridge, Mass.: Belknap.

Iser, Wolfgang
  1974   *The Implied Reader*. Baltimore: Johns Hopkins University Press.

Kelber, Werner H.
  1974   *The Kingdom in Mark: A New Place and a New Time*. Philadelphia: Fortress.

1983   *The Oral and the Written Gospel*. Philadelphia: Fortress Press.

Lord, Albert Bates
1960   *The Singer of Tales*. Cambridge, Mass.: Harvard University
            Press.

McLuhan, Marshall
1964   *Understanding Media: The Extensions of Man*. New York:
            McGraw-Hill.

Ong, Walter, J., S. J.
1967   *The Presence of the Word: Some Prolegomena for Cultural and
            Religious History* New Haven, Conn., Yale University Press.
1982   *Orality and Literacy*. New York: Methuen.

Rutherford, William G.
1905   *A Chapter in the History of Annotation*. Scholia Aristophanica,
            Vol. III. New York: Macmillan.

Scheub, Harold
1969   "The *Ntsomi: A Xhosa Performing Art*. Unpublished disserta-
            tion. University of Wisconsin.
1977   "Body and Image in Oral Narrative Performance," *New Literary
            History* 8: 345–67.

Silberman, Lou H.
1978   "'Habent Sua Fata Libelli': The Role of Wandering Themes in
            Some Hellenistic Jewish and Rabbinic Literature" in *The Rela-
            tionships Among the Gospels: An Interdisciplinary Dialogue*.
            Ed. William O. Walker. San Antonio: Trinity University Press.

Tannehill, Robert C.
1977   "The Disciples in Mark: The Function of a Narrative Role."
            Journal of Religion 57: 386–405.

FEED MY LAMBS: JOHN 21:15–19 AS ORAL GOSPEL

Gilbert L. Bartholomew
Lancaster Theological Seminary

ABSTRACT

Elocution is essential to meaning in human speech. The small degree to which it is represented in our writing system, the modern habit of silent reading, and the theological and aesthetic tradition of much of the Western church and academic community have conspired against attending to elocution as a serious exegetical problem in the study of Biblical texts.

Werner Kelber's *The Oral and the Written Gospel* is a milestone along the road of research into Biblical oral tradition. It should shock the modern reader into an awareness of how differently the stories in the Bible functioned in their original oral medium from the way they function as written texts today. But Kelber does not take into account the fact that in the ancient world written texts were normally read aloud.

The author of the present essay begins with the supposition that the Fourth Gospel would originally have been read aloud, and he seeks to answer the question; with what emotions would the Evangelist most likely have read Jesus' questions and Peter's answers in Jn 21:15–17? For evidence he looks to the Evangelist's explicit statement in v 17 that Peter was "grieved," and then to the immediate and wider narrative context of the conversation. He notes that clues to the original elocution may be clear, ambiguous, or non-existent. He concludes that the Evangelist most likely read Jesus' questions as moving from an initial to a deepening distress over the fact that Peter had denied him, and Peter's answers as moving from an initial shame at his denial of Jesus to a deepening shame that culminated in grief.

This conclusion about the emotions with which the Evangelist would seem to have read this conversation has important implications for the plot of the conversation, for the effect of hearing the conversation on the listeners, and for the listeners' theology of judgment and christology.

1. Introduction.

1.1   In treating human speech we cannot get away from the question of sound. For speech is fundamentally sound, and when speech is written down, it is certain aspects of the sound which are represented. The problem is that our writing system does not represent all the aspects of the sound which comprise speech. It does a good job with regard to the phonological aspects, namely the vowels and consonant which make up discrete words and which are then in turn combined into sentences and larger units of speech. But it does a very poor job representing the elocutionary aspects of speech. The various types of pauses are partially represented by the punctuation system, particularly those that come at the end of a clause. But many of the pauses that occur in the midst of a clause are not. Also the attitudes of question and exclamation are indicated in a general way, and occasionally emphasis is indicated by the use of italics. But emphasis is generally not represented at all, nor are there any devices for indicating variations in rate, rhythm, volume, and emotion.

1.2   Now there are aspects of phonology that are not represented; for example, all those things which combine to make up a particular accent. But these have little effect on the meaning. The elocutionary ingredients of the sound of speech which are poorly represented in the writing system, however, can endow the phonological elements with a great variety of possible meanings. George Bernard Shaw once said, "There are fifty ways of saying Yes, and five hundred of saying No, but only one way of writing them down" (quoted in Parish:59). This statement suggests the critical importance of elocution for meaning.

1.3   The purpose of this essay is to make a foray into the question of the original sound of the Fourth Gospel in respect to elocution, and particularly in respect to the emotional ingredients. The Western Church and community of scholars have inherited an elocutionary tradition which governs both our oral reading of scripture and the way we hear the sounds of the Bible in our imaginations when we are reading silently. But we are often only dimly aware of the elocutionary aspects of the texts we are reading. And when it does become the focus of our attention—often because someone speaks the words of the text in·a way which violate the tradition which we have inherited—we make our decisions almost always on the basis of theological (Bonhoeffer:56) or aesthetic preference (see below, pars. 5.1–2). Rarely do we make them on the basis of self-critical historical and exegetical study.[1] In what follows I shall examine the text of Jn 21:15–19 in its totality, for clues to how the redactor who is responsible for this little dialog intended his audience to hear it. In the course of this examination I hope to make clear the legitimacy and importance of the question of elocution for the Gospel's meaning, and both the possibility and difficulties of pursuing it.

2. The Scholarly Discussion

2.11   Description

I must begin by entering into a conversation with Werner Kelber's recent book, *The Oral and the Written Gospel* (1983). This work is perhaps the most serious and comprehensive attempt to deal with some Biblical texts in terms of the question of the medium of transmission and its effect on the message. Kelber begins with a consideration of the oral gospel tradition in contrast to the written Gospel of Mark. Then he turns his attention to the letters of Paul in order (1) to investigate the apostle's attitude towards oral speech in contrast to writing, (2) to explore the relationship between that attitude and some of the theological issues with which Paul struggles in his letters, and (3) to examine the relationship between Paul's oral gospel and his written letters as means of communication. I will be concerned here with what Kelber says about the written Gospel of Mark in contrast with the oral gospel tradition, and not with his discussion of Paul.

2.12   In speaking about Mark in writing in relation to the oral tradition, Kelber describes them as radically different. And he views this difference as a function of their respective medium—as he suggests in the title of his book, the "written," on the one hand, and the "oral," on the other. The oral tradition, he says, was transmitted through memory and by sound, in individual stories or sayings. It involved a coöperation between speaker and listeners that resulted in significant variation from one occasion of speaking to the next. Writing changed all this. Instead of memory and sound, the tradition was transmitted by silent text. Coöperation between hearers and a speaker was no longer a factor. Variation ceased, for writing froze into permanance a particular rendition of the story or saying. In addition, an extended narrative, comprehensive and consistent, became possible; indeed, Mark, for the first time, produced one such narrative.

2.13   This description of Mark that Kelber attributes to its being written instead of oral should as well apply to the other three Gospels, for they, too, have come down to us as written works. They can be thought of as fixed, *silent* versions of a gospel as well. If that is correct, then a foray into the elocutionary aspects of the *sound* of the Gospel of John which I propose to make is wholly inappropriate. And so, before I set out, I must try to show that Kelber's description of the character of a *written* Gospel is not correct.

2.21   Critique

The contrast which Kelber describes between the oral and the written gospel is right on target as far as a difference between two modes and uses of the gospel tradition is concerned. The drawing of that contrast is particularly helpful, because it brings to our attention a way of handling the gospel tradition wholly different from what we are accustomed to, and by doing so throws into sharp relief the way *we* tend to use that tradition. However, Kelber's description of what in fact did happen when the gospel was put into writing, as a necessary consequence of the change in medium, is clearly not correct.

2.22   He begins his first chapter with several quotations, the first of which is from John Gager's *Kingdom and Community:* "For apart from a consideration of its social setting, no statement about the origin and function of oral tradition may be accepted as valid."

The term "social setting," it is to be assumed, includes not only a particular community activity, like preaching or catechetical instruction, but also cultural characteristics of the community, for example, how texts were used generally throughout the culture. This statement ought to apply not only to any description of the origin and function of the oral tradition, but to that of the written tradition as well. Yet Kelber explicitly rejects the importance of social setting for understanding the gospel as written text. He says: "What characterizes orality in distinction from textuality is its intimate association with social life" (92). This is, however, simply not correct. While written texts can exist as objects apart from any social setting—as, for example, when they survive hidden in clay jars inside caves for thousands of years—they originate and function in particular social settings. We must, then, attend to the question of the original social setting of the Gospels as written texts. When we do, we come to a different view of their original function.

2.23   Ancient texts were used in such settings as communal worship, the school, and "publication." In these settings they were virtually always read *aloud*. The evidence for this is quite unequivocal. In fact, reading aloud in the ancient world was the general practice throughout the culture in any particular social setting, even that of private reading. The one famous exception we know about only proves the general rule.

2.231   Early evidence for reading aloud in the ancient world is found in the New Testament itself. In Acts 8:30 we are told that when Philip ran up to the chariot of the Ethiopian eunuch, he *"heard* him reading." Haenchen (1971) remarked on this, "The eunuch is reading aloud, as was usual in antiquity" (311). Then he added this note:

> This affirmation of Norden's (*Antike Kunstprosa*, 1898, 6) based on Augustine's *Confessions* VI.3, is wrongly contested by *Beg.* IV 96f. Billerbeck tells us (II, 687) that silent reading was forbidden among the Jews. The commentators who provided the eunuch with a companion to read to him were as yet unacquainted with Norden's discovery.

2.2321   This brings us to the very interesting passage in Augustine's *Confessions* VI.3:

> When [Ambrose] was not with [crowds of busy men]. . . , he either refreshed his body with needed food or his mind with

reading. When he read, his eyes moved down the pages and his heart sought out their meaning, while his voice and tongue remained silent. Often when we were present . . . we saw him reading to himself and never otherwise. . . . We thought that in that short time which he obtained for refreshing his mind, free from the din of other men's problems, he did not want to be summoned to some other matter. We thought too that perhaps he was afraid, if the author he was reading had expressed things in an obscure manner, then it would be necessary to explain it for some perplexed but eager listener, or to discuss some more difficult questions, and if his time were used up in such tasks, he would be able to read fewer books than he wished to. However, need to save his voice, which easily grew hoarse, was perhaps the correct reason why he read to himself. But with whatever intention he did it, that man did it for a good purpose.

2.2322   To this passage, the translator of the above quotation, John K. Ryan appends the note:

> It was the ancient custom to read out loud and in company with others. Augustine has already given an instance of this when he tells how he and Faustus read together. The present passage is reported to be one of the few descriptions of silent reading in ancient literature. The detail with which Augustine describes St. Ambrose's custom indicates how unusual silent reading must have been. (385)

2.233   Further statements to this effect are frequent in scholarly literature. In *A History of Education in Antiquity*, Henri I. Marrou says, "The child read aloud, of course: throughout antiquity, until the late Empire, silent reading was exceptional. People read aloud to themselves, or, if they could, got a servant to read to them." (154) and Geo Widengren, in an article, "Oral Tradition and Written Literature," says "it is wrong to contrast oral and written tradition too much in ancient Semitic culture. . . . Writing down is codified oral tradition, and as such primarily intended to be read aloud, to be recited." (212)

2.234   When we look at the primary evidence provided by the ancient sources, we find frequent indications that texts were read aloud. See, for example, all the passages, both Biblical and non-Biblical, cited in Bauer's lexicon where *anaginōskō* clearly means "read aloud." I have checked all the texts available to me which Bauer cites in his first paragraph, where he gives the translation "read," rather than "read aloud." In those passages there is simply no indication of the manner in which the reading was done. There is nothing to suggest that it was done in silence. See also Bultmann's article on *anaginōskō* in TDNT (1964: 343–4).

2.241   This evidence for the virtually unexceptional reading aloud of texts in the ancient world[2] makes it clear that Kelber cannot be correct in saying that Mark has silenced the voices of the oral tradition. First, it is quite true that, as marks on a writing surface, they *are* silent. But as marks which constituted words for an ancient reader, they fostered sound.

2.242   Secondly, as marks on a writing surface texts also made possible a transformation of verbal communication from an interchange between two living human beings to an interchange between an inanimate object (a book) and a reader. But as texts read aloud in social situations where there were listeners, the words which the texts transmitted were restored to a context of live performance.

2.243   Thirdly, as marks on a writing surface, texts also froze the words of the tradition according to a particular rendition of it.[3] And they deprived those who listened to them being read aloud from participating in the process of composition,[4] but only as far as shifts and alterations of the words themselves were concerned. When those words embodied in the text were spoken aloud once again in the presence of hearers, coöperation between speaker and listeners would have continued necessarily, if the words of the reader were to have any meaning for those who listened. The job of actualizing that meaning simply became more difficult because the means had become limited. The speaker was no longer free to respond to the listeners' mood or inattention by altering the words, but had to depend solely on such elements of speech as emotion, pause, and gesture.

2.244   Finally, as marks on a writing surface, the texts made it possible for the words of the tradition to "become visible and knowlable apart from sound and hearing." (92) That is the way that many biblical texts become known to us today. While in the ancient world it was certainly *possible* for the tradition to become known in that way, the evidence indicates that it *did not* become known in that way. In the ancient world the words which the biblical texts offered were, to a very great extent, known first to people as spoken words, that is, as words spoken to them by another person who was reading aloud, in communal worship, for example. Only later would they have come to read the texts themselves. That is still often true today. Many people have heard at least portions of the Bible read to them before they themselves learned to read those passages.

2.245   Written texts, then, silenced the language of the gospel only insofar as they are made up of visible marks on a writing surface which in and of themselves have no sound whatsoever. When they were taken up and read aloud, the language they conveyed was not devoid of sound. In contrast to the configuration of elements constituting what we term the "oral tradition," written texts stood in opposition *only* to *memory* as a means of transmission, *not* to *sound*.

2.3   It is quite appropriate, then, for me to raise the question of the originally intended sound of the words of the Fourth Gospel in respect to elocution. In fact, it appears to be a methodological necessity to raise this question, if we wish to make progress in our effort to understand the Gospels as they were understood by their original audiences. This latter claim remains to be demonstrated, no doubt. It may by no means be obvious to a modern person that elocution is a decisive factor in the meaning of language. For we have been getting along for years reading the Bible without paying any attention to the question of proper elocution. In the course of discussing this aspect of the original sound of Jn 21:15–19, consequently, I will be especially interested in the question: what difference will one way of speaking the words make for meaning as opposed to another?

In setting out on this investigation into the elocution of the Fourth Gospel, we face a major obstacle: The texts possess a paucity of clues to the original elocution of the words. They were not originally intended for readers who had never before heard anyone read them aloud. Yet, now that we are long divorced from the tradition of reading aloud which was the original context for the passing on of the texts, we have little to go on apart from the texts, in spite of the fact that those texts are not adequate to meet our need.

3.   John 21:15–19

3.1   Literary structure and content.

3.11   We now turn to the text of Jn 21:15–19. What sort of oral rendition does the text itself encourage us to give to its words? Before we can begin to answer that question, we must attend to the literary structure and the content of those verses.

3.12   From the point of view of literary structure, v 15 begins a new unit. A new scene begins with a new indication of time ("When they had eaten breakfast"), and the rest of the disciples disappear into the background as the spotlight focuses on Jesus and Peter alone. This scene continues through v 19, after which a new character, the Beloved Disciple, comes on stage and introduces a new element into the conversation.

3.13   Vv 15–17

3.131   Vv 15–19 consist of four clear parts: v 15, v 16, v 17, and vv 18–19. The first three of these parts are parallel to each other, each containing a question, an answer, and an exhortation. There are two verbal ways in which these parallel elements differ from one another. 1) *Omission and addition*. In v 15 Jesus states his question in terms of a comparison ("more than these"), while in vv 16 and 17 the comparison is absent. In vv 15 and 16 Peter's answer is introduced simply by the words, "he said to him," whereas in v 17 the narrator adds a comment informing us of how Peter felt and then adds a clause to Peter's answer. 2) *Substitution of one word for another. Phileō* parallels *agapaō; ginōskō, oida; poimainō, boskō;* and *probaton* and/or *probation, arnion*.[5] What sort of movement is dictated by these changes from one parallel element to the next? I shall discuss the significance of the omission and the additions below. Here it is necessary to say something about the alternation between *agapaō* and *phileō*.[6]

3.132   Most ancient Greek commentators and Reformation scholars, as well as of most present-day commentators regard these two verbs as synonymous in the Fourth Gospel (Barrett: 486; Bernard: 702–4; Brown: 1103; Bultmann, 1971:711, n.5; Hoskyns: 558; Schnackenburg, 1982:363). But British scholars of the last century (Brown[7] lists Trench, Westcott, and Plummer), as well as several present-day commentators (Marsh; Brown names Evans) and translators (J. B. Phillips), argue for a clear distinction between them. Some, in accord with the earlier, classical usage, see in *phileō* a higher form of love than in *agapaō*. Others argue for the reverse relationship between the two.

3.133   I think it is wrong to maintain a distinction between these two verbs in this passage with regard to the kind of love to which they refer. In other clearly parallel passages, the Fourth Evangelist uses them interchangeably. I cite only two examples. In 14:23 and in 16:27 Jesus teaches his disciples that, if a person loves him, the Father will love that person in turn. In the former passage the verb is *agapaō* and in the latter *phileō*. Likewise the Beloved Disciple is described as such using both verbs: in 20:2 using *phileō*, and in 13:23; 19:26; 21:7, 20 using *agapaō*.

3.134   In addition to this parallel use of *agapaō* and *phileō*, there is another passage in which nouns deriving from the same root as these two verbs are defined in terms of each other. In 15:13 Jesus teaches that the greatest love *(agapē)* which a person can express is to "lay down his life for his friends (philōn)." We shall see below that the reason Jesus is questioning Peter's love in 21:15–19 is precisely because Peter had promised to lay down his life for Jesus (13:37) and had failed to live up to that promise (18:15–18, 25–27). Therefore, when 15:9–15 is part of the context of our reading or hearing of 21:15–17, the use of both *agapaō* and *phileō* in the latter passage may prompt us to recall that, in the teaching Jesus gave to his disciples the night before he died, he defined both "love" and "friendship" in terms of being willing to lay down one's life.[8]

3.135   It was necessary to clarify the relationship of *agapaō* and *phileō* in 21:15–17 in order to describe the literary structure of that conversation. The fact that they are synonymous means that the content of Jesus question to Peter does not change at v 17 with regard to the kind of love he has in mind. Rather, the question remain the same throughout the entire sequence, except for the dropping of the comparison after v 15. He asks the same question *for* the third time; he does not alter the question *on* the third time. (Schnackenburg, 1982:362). Likewise Peter's pain after Jesus' third question results not from an alteration in Jesus' question from one kind of "love" to another. He is pained because Jesus asks him the *same* question *for* the third time, after he has already answered Jesus twice in the affirmative! In other words, there is only one real question in this little conversation between Jesus and Peter, and Jesus is not satisfied with Peter's answer to that question until the end of v 17, after which he lays it to rest.

3.14   Vv 18–19

3.141   Vv 18–19 are integrally related to vv 15–17, much more so than is apparent in the text of those verses. We shall see that shortly. Meanwhile, let us look closely at vv 18–19.

3.142   In vv 18–19 Jesus prophesies Peter's death. He does so, first by means of the metaphor of an old man being dressed by another and led around against his will (v 18), and then by explicit statement: "This he said in order to show by what death he would glorify God" (v 19). The explicit statement echoes Jesus' words about his own coming death in 12:33; and indeed, the figure of the old man stretching out his hands calls to mind the cross.

3.143   When Jesus then concludes his prophecy with the command, "Follow me," he is using a word which the Gospel context has loaded with very specific meaning, namely, follow *to death!* For in 13:37 Peter vowed that he would "follow" Jesus to the point that "I will lay down my life for you."

3.1431   This command of Jesus, "Follow me," in fact, brings to completion a major sequence in the Fourth Gospel which began in 13:36. There Jesus said to Peter, "Where I am going you can*not* follow me *now; but* you shall follow *afterward*." To that Peter responded, "Lord, why can I not follow you now? I will lay down my life for you." To that Jesus in turn replied, "Will you lay down your life for me? Truly, truly, I tell you, the cock will not crow, before you deny me three times" (13:36–38).

3.1432   Jesus' prophecy, "you can*not* follow me *now*," is, then, fulfilled in the story of Peter's denial (18:15–18, 25–27). For there Peter does the opposite of what he vowed. Instead of following Jesus "now" and laying down his life for him, he denies that he is one of Jesus' disciples.

3.1433   In 21:15–19, then, it is "afterward." Jesus said in 13:36, "you shall follow *afterward*." And so, in 21:19, after prophesying Peter's death, first by an image, and then by explicit statement, both of which connect Peter's death with Jesus' own, Jesus now commands him to follow, and indeed follow him to death, as Peter promised he would in 13:37. Thus Jesus points to the fulfillment of his promise to Peter in 13:36, namely, "You shall follow afterward."

3.15   The Relationship between vv 15–17 and 18–19

3.151   What do vv 15–17 have to do with all of this? The words in those verses are also loaded with connotations of death. First of all, in vv 15–17 Jesus repeatedly asks Peter, "Do you love me?" What does it mean to love in the Fourth Gospel? According to the Supper Discourse, one thing it means is to keep Jesus' commandments (14:15; 15:10); but it comes to greatest expression when a person "lays down his life for his friends" (15:13)—the very thing Peter vowed to do for Jesus in 13:37 and failed to do for him in 18:15–18, 25–27, and the thing which would have set him apart as loving Jesus "more than these [others love him]: (21:15). (See below, par. 3.2331.)

3.152   Secondly, when Peter protests that Jesus already knows the answer to the question he is asking in 21:15–17, Jesus instructs him to feed (boske) / tend (poimaine) his lambs (arnia) / sheep (probata and/or probatia). And what does it mean to be a good shepherd (poimēn) in the Fourth Gospel? "The good shepherd lays down his life for the sheep" (10:11; cf. 10:15)!

3.153   This, then, is the connotation which has accrued to the word "love" and to the phrase "feed my sheep" from earlier parts of the Gospel. While a person reading or hearing these words apart from that context would not suspect that they have to do with Peter's death, one who has been attentive to the foregoing parts of the story could be expected to be well aware of them.[9]

3.2   Elocution.
3.21   Introduction.
3.211   Given the meaning of Jn 21:15–19 within the larger context of the Fourth Gospel, let us now turn to the question of the original sound of the words in respect to elocution.

3.212   The text of Jn 21:15–19, together with the larger context in which it is found, provide us with a variety of clues to the original sound. These take the form of 1) direct statements, 2) the structure and substance of 21:15–19, and 3) the structure and substance of the larger narrative. They range across a wide spectrum, from the absence of any sort of clue on the one end, through clues of greater and lesser ambiguity in the middle, to rather precise clues on the other end. We no doubt may wish that the set of these clues were fuller than it is, and that some of those clues that are provided were less ambiguous than they are. Yet they do point us in a certain direction.

3.213   What are the clues to the original elocution of Jn 21:15–19? In what follows I shall limit my attention to Jesus' questions and Peter's answers in vv 15–17 and to one aspect of their elocution, namely, the attitude or emotion appropriate to them. Within the space of an article, an adequate discussion of those matters is a large enough task.

3.22   The words of Peter.
3.221   Common oral interpretations.
There is one explicit clue in this story as to how a character felt when he spoke: "Peter was grieved[10]. . . . And he said. . . ." (v17). What are Peter's emotions in the story prior to this third protestation of love for Jesus? The oral interpreters I have heard read this story aloud have read

the first two protestations in a rather matter-of-fact or objective way,[11] or with a tone of warm assurance, or in a way that suggests that Peter was puzzled that Jesus should even ask about his love.[12]

3.222   In light of the fact there are no explicit clues to Peter's attitude in these first two responses to Jesus' question, we turn both to the whole of 21:15–19 and to the Gospel's larger narrative context for help. We shall first ask how these three possible interpretations of Peter's emotion fit into that larger context. Then we shall ask whether any other possibilities suggest themselves.

3.223   Common oral interpretations and the plot of the Gospel.

Looking at the larger story of Peter in the Fourth Gospel, we see that in 21:15–19 we have the first face to face encounter between Jesus and Peter since Peter's denial that he was one of Jesus' disciples—a denial made in the wake of a promise that he would follow Jesus to the point of laying down his life for Jesus. How do the three possible attitudes of Peter mentioned above (matter-of-fact, warmly assuring, puzzled) fit into that narrative context? They all have a similar effect on the plot of Peter's story. They portray Peter as one who is utterly unaware of the disgraceful nature of the act he performed. The plot of the conversation narrated in 21:15–19, then, must achieve a twofold end. It must 1) move Peter from a broken relationship with Jesus, brought about by his denial that he was one of Jesus' disciples, to a restored relationship. But in order to accomplish that, it must 2) also move him from a *lack of awareness* of what he did in denying Jesus to a recognition of his deed and to grief over what he had done (v 17).

3.224   An alternative oral interpretation and the plot.

All three interpretations of Peter's attitude in these first two responses to Jesus I have mentioned thus far, affect the plot of the larger narrative about Peter in the same way. But these three are not the only possible attitudes with which those words of Peter may have been spoken. In the larger narrative context of the Fourth Gospel, yet another way of speaking those first two responses becomes possible; namely, an attitude of deep shame, arising out of Peter's *complete awareness* of what he did in the courtyard of the high priest.[13] This attitude results in a different plot for vv 15–17 from the one described above. What begins as a feeling of shame intensifies, as the conversation moves along through Jesus' second and third putting of the question, until it culminates in the intense "grief" reported explicitly by the narrator in v 18. Peter does not need to overcome a lack of awareness of what he did. As in the synoptic gospels, he was only too aware of his failure from the moment of his third denial. Thus his relationship to Jesus only needs to be restored.

3.225   The portrayal of Peter in the Gospel as a whole.

3.2251   Which of these oral interpretations of Peter's attitude at the begininng of this conversation with Jesus fit with the way Peter is characterized throughout the Fourth Gospel? In that larger context, Peter is portrayed as anything but perfect. In addition to his cowardly failure in the courtyard of the high priest to live up to his promise to follow Jesus to death (18:15–18, 25–27), he is eager beyond his ability to fulfil (13:36–8; 21:15 ["more than these"]). He misunderstands Jesus (13:6–11; 18:10–11), or he lacks the understanding of the Beloved Disciple (20:8, 21:7).

3.2252   But for all the negative elements in the way the Fourth Evangelist portrays him, Peter is basically a sympathetic character. At the beginning of the Gospel he is the one whom Jesus calls "Rock" (1:42). At a critical point in Jesus' ministry, when many of his disciples abandon him, it is Peter who says, "Lord, to whom shall we go? You have the words of eternal life" (6:68). At the end of the Evangelist's story, Peter is the one whom Jesus, through this confrontation in 21:15ff, summons to be faithful to his promise to die as Jesus' follower, out of love for Jesus and as the shepherd of his sheep.

3.2253   Even Peter's misunderstandings and failures to understand are shortcomings with which a reader or hearer of the Fourth Gospel could easily sympathize. First, in 13:6–11 Jesus proposes to do something for Peter which is quite offensive to the cultural norms of the time. Footwashing was something an inferior always did for a social better. Slaves did it for their masters, wives did it for their husbands, and disciples did it for their teachers. (See Barrett: 366, for the evidence.) Second, in 18:10–11, although Jesus reprimands him, Peter has acted very courageously in the face of a great host of enemies. Third, even Peter's denial of Jesus is understandable as a failure of nerve in the face of the real possibility of death. At least he had the courage to follow Jesus into the courtyard of the high priest. How many readers and listeners would have been confident that they would have done even that well?

3.2254   Nor do the contrasts between Peter and the Beloved Disciple work against the sympathetic portrayal of Peter. The Evangelist's report in 20:8 that "he [the Beloved Disciple] saw and believed," together with the subsequent explanation that "they did not yet understand the scripture that he must rise from the dead," suggests that the Beloved Disciple is being set in contrast to all the disciples and not just to Peter. The same is certainly true in 21:7, where only the Beloved Disciple recognizes Jesus. It is not that Peter and the others are so dull, but that the Beloved Disciple is so exceptional.

3.2255   All these things incline the readers or listeners to a sympathetic relationship with Peter. In contrast, to portray Peter as matter-of-fact or warmly assuring or puzzled, and therefore as unaware of his three denials of Jesus, when he, in 21:15–17, for the first time encounters Jesus face to face after Jesus' death and resurrection, would be to portray him in a very unsympathetic light. What normal person who has treated a beloved friend as Peter did in the high priest's courtyard would not be burdened with remorse and shame?

3.226 Conclusion.

3.2261 It seems to me, then, that to endow the words of Peter in Jn 21:15 and 16 with a matter-of-fact attitude, or an attitude of warm assurance or of puzzlement would be out of keeping with the sympathetic portrayal of Peter in the larger Gospel narrative. Only a sense of deep shame at denying Jesus, especially in the wake of his boast that he would lay down his life for Jesus, would preserve him in a sympathetic light.

3.2262 Whether or not others agree with this judgment, I hope that it will at least be clear to them how important it is to the meaning of 21:15–19 whether we hear the words of Peter with one emotion or with another. The very plot of the conversation is affected by Peter's attitude.

3.23 The questions asked by Jesus.

3.231 We now turn to the questions which Jesus puts to Peter. With what emotion or emotions did the original narrator most likely interpret those questions? I have heard readers speak them either in a completely objective way or with a warm and gentle understanding or a mild sadness. Here the Evangelist give us no explicit information such as he gives us for the words of Peter when he tells us that Peter was "grieved." We are left to rely solely on whatever clues are offered by the structure and substance of both the immediate and the broader context.

3.232 The name "Simon son of John."

3.2321 Let us begin by considering the name by which Jesus addresses Peter in his questions. All three times in Jn 21:15–17, Jesus calls Peter "Simon, son of John."[14] In discussing the significance of this name, three scholars comment explicitly on the attitude which they think it implies. Lindars says that "the use of the patronymic adds solemnity to the address" (633). Brown observes that Jesus is "treating him less familiarly" (1102). And Schnackenburg renders the negative judgment that "a cool attitude of Jesus cannot be read out from the form of the address " (1982: 362). Closer examination of this name is required.

3.2322 The only other time Jesus addresses Peter by name in the entire Fourth Gospel is in 1:42. There also he calls him, "Simon, son of John."[15] But immediately he goes on to give him the name "Cephas," which the narrator explains means "Peter" ("Rock"). What are we to make of the fact that in 21:15–17 Jesus does not call this disciple by the nickname Cephas or Peter that he gave him at the beginning of their relationship? Is Jesus being solemn, or unfriendly or cool towards Peter?

3.2323 Both Bultmann (1971: 101) and Schnackenburg (1968: 311–13) note that Jesus says, "You *shall* be called (*klēthēsē*) Cephas," and understand the future tense to mean that Jesus is not giving him a new name immediately but only prophesying that he shall be called by a new name in the future. In that case the answer to our question would seem to be that we should not *expect* Jesus to call Peter by his nickname in 21:15–17. The time has not yet arrived for him to be called by it. If this is so, then the fact that Jesus does not call this disciple "Peter" here would not imply that Jesus is being unfriendly or cool.

3.2324   Against this view, Brown (80) observes that "the future tense is part of the literary style of name changing." He cites the LXX in Gen 17:5 and 15 (*klēthēsetai to onoma sou/autēs* instead of *klēthēsē*). Gen 17:5, where God says to Abram, "Your name shall no longer be called Abram, but your name shall be Abraham," is the watershed in the narrative between the use of the two names. And both the narrator (17:9) and God (22:1) address Abraham by the new name from that point on. The same is true of 17:15 in regard to the names Sarai and Sarah.[16] The situation is a bit different in the Fourth Gospel in regard to the use of the names Simon and Peter. In contrast to the narrator in Genesis, in the Fourth Gospel the Evangelist refers to "the brother of Simon *Peter*" already in 1:40 before Jesus gives him the new name. And, although in Genesis God as well as the narrator call Abraham and Sarah by their new names, between 1:42 and 21:15, *Jesus* nowhere addresses Peter by any name whatever. Only the Evangelist refers to him by name. And the name he uses is consistently either Peter or Simon Peter. But that is exactly where the evidence of the LXX use of *klēthēsetai*) comes to our aid. The use of the new names by God as well as by the narrator after Gen 17:5 and 15 makes it clear that the new name becomes effective immediately, even if the character is not addressed by it.

3.2325   Here at the end of the Gospel, then, it must be that Jesus departs from using the name Peter for some other reason other than that "will be called" refers to some time later than the time of Jesus' final conversation with Peter. And the most fitting explanation for the fact that Jesus calls this disciple "Simon, son of John" is that, in denying Jesus, Simon did not live up to this nickname, and it would therefore have been most inappropriate for Jesus to use it.

3.2326   But can we go beyond this and say that the name "Simon, son of John" implies that Jesus is being solemn, or unfriendly or cool towards Peter? Commentators appropriately note that the Fourth Evangelist offers no explanation of why Jesus gave Simon the nickname "Peter." This contrasts with Mt 16:18, where Matthew tells us that Peter would be the rock on which the church would be founded. (Brown: 80; Schnackenburg, 1968: 312-13). However, there is also wide agreement among commentators that in the Fourth Gospel Jesus gives Simon this nickname either as an estimate of his character[17], or as an indication of the role he would play in the future, or both.[18] Jesus' use of the name "Simon, son of John" and his avoidance of the name "Peter," then, is appropriate to, and even points to, Peter's denial of Jesus, by which he failed to live up to the character and role signified by that name.[19]

3.2327 This means that it is not enough to say with Lindars that "the use of the patronymic adds solemnity to the address" (633). It also confronts Peter with his failure. But there would also seem to be no warrant for Brown's view that, by not using the name "Peter" Jesus is "treating him less familiarly" (1102). I at least have found no evidence that the nickname was indicative of the special relationship between Jesus and Peter as well as of Jesus' estimate of Peter's character and the role that he would play. So far as the name goes, Schnackenburg's negative assessment of its value as a clue to Jesus' attitude would seem to be the best: "a cool attitude of Jesus cannot be read out from the form of address" (1982: 362).

3.233 The content of Jesus' questions

3.2331 We turn, then, to the content of Jesus' questions, to see whether that provides us with any clues to Jesus' attitude in asking them. Jesus' first way of stating his question to Peter is: "Do you love me *more than these?*" These words would seem to be a taunt. "More than these" is an ambiguous phrase. (See Brown: 1103–4, in regard to the alternatives.) But it surely means, "more than these *others love me.*" For there would be no reason for Jesus to be asking Peter whether he loves Jesus more than *he loves* these *other disciples* or whether he loves Jesus more than *he loves* this *fishing gear.* There is no hint in the Fourth Gospel that Peter is struggling between being loyal to Jesus and loyalty to the other disciples or between staying with Jesus and going back to his former career. In Jn 21:3 he seems to decide to go fishing simply because he is at a loss for what else to do. There is, however, a perfectly good reason why Jesus would be asking Peter whether he loves him more than these *other disciples love him.* For Peter had made a singular promise to follow Jesus to the point of laying down his life for him—and he failed to do that! So a taunt is certainly in order on Jesus' part.

3.2332 When we turn to the way Jesus puts his question to Peter the second and third time, we note that these latter two times Jesus asks whether Peter loves him *at all, without comparison* with anyone else's love. That is a more painful question, and in the context it is an even sharper taunt.

3.2333 Thus there is an increase in the intensity from Jesus' first asking of his question to the second, corresponding to the increase in intensity of feeling from an initial shame to grief which we found in the succeeding answers which Peter gives. We might reasonably assume from this that the original narrator spoke Jesus third question with greater urgency yet. This would, however, have been achieved by his voice alone and not by any change in the wording.[20]

3.2334 But if we try to go beyond this and identify Jesus' precise attitude in asking this taunting question, the most we can say is that complete detachment, or neutrality, or objectivity would seem to be

ruled out. There must be at least an increase in the intensity with which
Jesus asks the question. But the formulation of the questions and the
development from one to the other provide no more positive clue to
Jesus' attitude than did the name, "Simon, son of John." We could still
conceive of Jesus' speaking with a variety of other possible attitudes. He
may have felt the mild sadness with which I have often heard readers
speak his words, or possibly warm understanding. The latter feeling is
suggested, perhaps, by the fact that Jesus' knew ahead of time that Peter
would deny him. Or Jesus may have spoken with icy sternness, or pained
disappointment, feelings which would be quite appropriate in light of
what Peter did to Jesus in the high priest's courtyard. We step back,
then, from our close-up examination of Jn 21:15–17 to take into account
the Gospel as a whole. Is there any help available from a study of that
wider context?

3.234   Jesus' emotions and attitudes in the Gospel context.

3.2341   Introduction.

3.23411   To ask with what attitude the original narrator might have spoke
Jesus' questions in the light of his presentation of Jesus in the Fourth
Gospel as a whole is to raise a question which demands the same sort of
verse by verse detailed analysis as I am presenting here for Jn 21:15–17.
And so what follows here must be viewed strictly as a preliminary survey,
to be tested critically at every point, and to be enlarged through a
consideration of passages not discussed here.

3.23412   In *Anatomy of the Fourth Gospel*, R. Alan Culpepper offers a
survey of Jesus' emotions and motives (109–112). This survey includes
various categories of data. First, there are the Evangelist's *descriptions* of
Jesus' emotions and his reports of *words* or *actions* of Jesus which express
or exhibit clear emotions. Secondly, there a reports of Jesus' responses to
human needs and requests. And thirdly, there are stories of his encounters with people who respond to him in a variety of ways (positively,
negatively, inadequately, unfaithfully) and to whom he responds in turn.
The first and third categories here are most pertinent for the present
study. We need to know generally what emotions the Jesus of the Fourth
Gospel is capable of exhibiting (first category). And, since our present
concern is how Jesus might be reacting to the fact that Peter denied him,
we need to know his responses to the way people other than Peter related
to and behaved towards him (third category).

3.2342   Explicit indications of emotion.

We begin with the emotions which the Evangelist indicates explicitly. In
numerous passages, using both the words *agapaō* and *phileō* the Evangelist speaks of Jesus' love for various people or for God. In addition to
this attitude, he reports several others. In 2:13–22 he tells a story in
which Jesus acts violently and he describes that violence as the result of
zeal. In 2:24 he attributes to Jesus an attitude of distrust. In 6:11 he says

that Jesus gave thanks to God, and in 11:41 Jesus himself expresses thanks to God. In 11:33 he says that Jesus *enebrimēsatō tō pneumati*, and 11:38 he describes him as *embrimōmenos en heautō*. There is dispute over exactly what the verb *embrimaomai* connotes—is there anger involved or not?—and to what it is a response; but a strong emotion is clearly involved. (See, for example, Brown: 425–6; Barrett: 332; Hoskyns: 403–5.) The verb *tarassō* is also used of Jesus in several places (11:33; 12:27; 13:21). It also signifies a strong emotion, and it is variously translated "troubled" (Hoskyns: 398; Bauer; RSV), "shuddered" (Brown: 426), "deeply moved" (NEB), "in great distress" (JB); or it is described as meaning "a fearful perturbation" (Barrett: 332). In 11:15; 15:11; and 17:13 Jesus himself speaks of his joy (*chairō* or *chara*). And finally, in 11:35 the Evangelist tells us that Jesus wept (*edakrysen*). This is a short list. But even by itself it shows that the Fourth Evangelist's Jesus does not go through the Gospel in a constant state of detachment and reserve. He exhibits a healthy range of strong emotions: love, zeal, distrust, thankfulness, possibly anger, deep distress of some sort, joy, and grief.

3.2343   Jesus' attitudes in his encounters with others.

3.23431   Next we examine Jesus' encounters with others, in which he reacts to their enthusiasm, faith, failures, or hostility. In these passages there is no explicit indication of his emotions, and we must deduce them from what he says and does. Space prohibits a discussion all these encounters. The most fruitful to attend to are some of those in which people attracted to Jesus either exhibit an inadequate faith or fail him in some way.

3.23432   We look first at two instances of Jesus' response to inadequate faith. Nicodemus was attracted to Jesus because of his signs (3:2). We know from 2:23–25 that faith based on the seeing of Jesus' signs is not to be trusted. Nicodemus comes to Jesus apparently to get some questions answered. How does Jesus respond? He challenges him with a description of adequate faith, apparently before Nicodemus even has a chance to say all that is on his mind. He is in no way careful not to destroy what faith Nicodemus does have. He exhibits no sympathy for Nicodemus' problems of belief. On the contrary, he chides Nicodemus with words which the Evangelist suggest a tone of ridicule and sarcasm[21]: "You are a teacher of Israel and do not understand these things?!" (3:10)

3.23433   The royal official was also attracted to Jesus (4:46–54). In 4:48 Jesus responds to the man's request to heal his son with the words, "Unless you see signs and wonders, you will not believe." Even though these words refer to the people generally (second person plural), they suggest that Jesus viewed the man's faith as a response to his signs and therefore, like Nicodemus', inadequate. What is the character of Jesus' response in 4:48? Lindars (203), on the one hand, calls it "a slight rebuff." But Schnackenburg (1968: 466) speaks of the "grave doubt expressed by

Jesus *(ou mē)*." In classical Greek, *ou mē* with the aorist subjunctive is "the most definite form of negation regarding the future. This mode of expression is more common in the NT and for the most part less emphatic than in the classical language." (Blass: §365) But there are a number of NT instances where the expression is quite capable of bearing the emphasis which it has in classical Greek (Moulton: 189), and the NT use must be judged on a case by case basis. In 4:48 the emphasis would certainly be appropriate. And Moulton cites two other instances in the Fourth Gospel where he says the emphatic force of *ou mē* is "most obvious" (189). One cannot rule out Lindars' view here, so it is possible that Jesus' words in 4:48 were spoken in a mildly critical tone. But the Evangelist may also have spoken them with an attitude of exasperation.

3.23434   We now turn from instances of Jesus' responses to inadequate faith to passages in which he responds to some failure on the part of one of the twelve. There is one passage in which the Evangelist reports explicitly Jesus' reaction to a failure on the part of a disciple. In 13:21, at the supper table Jesus foretells his betrayal by one of his own. The Evangelist says that, before Jesus spoke of it, *etarachthē tō pneumati*. In our discussion above of the Evangelist's explicit indications of Jesus' feelings, we noted that the verb is variously translated but denotes some form of deep distress.

3.23435   Later during that same supper Peter enthusiastically vows that he will lay down his life for Jesus (13:37). Jesus does not receive Peter's promise with equal enthusiasm. Nor does he do anything to encourage Peter. On the contrary, he asks whether Peter will really do what he says, and then makes the painful prediction that Peter will in fact do the opposite. Now there is no explicit indication of his attitude in asking that question and making that prediction. I have often heard it read in a tone of deep sadness. But in content it is a very cutting question, and that suggests more of a biting or ridiculing tone of voice.

3.23436   Shortly after the conversation involving Peter's vow to lay down his life for Jesus, Philip asks Jesus, "Lord, show us the Father." Jesus replies, "Have I been with you for such a long time, and you do not recognize me, Philip? The one who has seen me has seen the Father. How can you say, 'Show us the Father'?" (14:8–9) These words suggest an attitude of distress and impatience.

3.235   Results of survey for Jn 21:15–17.

3.2351   The aim of this survey of Jesus' emotions and his attitudes towards others in the Fourth Gospel has been to establish the boundaries within which the oral interpretation of Jesus' questions to Peter in 21:15–17 must be carried out. First of all, we have seen that, despite the paucity of explicit indications of Jesus' feelings in the Gospel, those that do exist range across the spectrum of human emotions and in some instances are clearly quite intense. Second, in instances other than 21:15–17 in which

Jesus is reacting to the inadequacies and failures of person who are positively disposed towards him, his words in no way suggest an attitude of cool, objective assessment on his part. Nor does he display sympathy with their weaknesses or an appreciation of the bit of faith they do have and a desire not to damage whatever is there lest it too be destroyed. He swiftly and uncompromisingly challenges whatever is wrong. His words are critical, sometimes sarcastic, and sometimes suggest an attitude of distress and even exasperation.

3.2352   The content of Jesus' questions to Peter in 21:15–17 shows an increase in the intensity of the taunt from the first to the second question. That in itself suggests cool objectivity is not an appropriate interpretation of Jesus' attitude towards Peter. The variety of emotions shown by the above survey to belong to the character of Jesus in the Fourth Gospel encourage us to follow the lead of that increased intensity of the taunt and consider attitudes more appropriate to it.

3.2353   It is also clear that Jesus is not warm and understanding of Peter's act of denial. His words to Peter in 21:15–17 give no hint of sympathy. On the contrary, his words contain a clear taunt. In addition, the above survey of Jesus' responses to the inadequate faith and failures of those attracted to him show that he several times speaks in a way that suggest not gentle understanding but some degree of distress, including possibly exasperation and even biting sarcasm.

3.2353   If, then, Jesus' questions to Peter are spoken by the oral interpreter in a biting way, with an increasing degree of distress, matching the sharpening of the taunt, that would fit the way Jesus is presented elsewhere in the Fourth Gospel. It would also work together well with the initial feeling of shame on Peter's part increasing to grief in his third answer. An attitude of warm assurance, in contrast, would not fit well with Peter's responses at all. If that were Jesus' attitude, Peter's initial feeling of shame would more likely subside than intensify.

4.   Conclusions.

4.1   The difficulty, legitimacy, and necessity of oral interpretation.

I have now discussed the clues to the original locutionary quality of the words of Jesus' questions and Peter's answer in Jn 21:15–17. To what conclusions does this discussion lead? First of all, it is surely clear by now how *difficult* it is to deal with the question of the original elocution of the Gospels when they were read aloud. There is a paucity of evidence, and what evidence exists is usually more or less ambiguous. But although it is clear that the question of the original oral interpretation is a difficult one, I hope that it is also now clear that it is both *legitimate* and *essential* to pursue it. To begin with, the difficulty of dealing with the question is no different than the problem we have in dealing with any other exegetical question. The evidence is always sparse and ambiguous. Secondly, the emotions and other elocutionary dimensions of speech with which the words of the text are endowed is an unavoidable ingredient in the *meaning* of the text.

4.2   Plot.

We have seen how important the attitude which Peter exhibits in speaking to Jesus is to the *plot* of the conversation. Does Jesus first have to jog Peter's memory of his denials before he can call him to fulfill his promise to follow Jesus to death? Or is Peter already all too painfully aware of what he has done? And do Jesus' questions function to bring about in Peter a full and honest facing of the gravity of what he has done in the presence of the one he has wronged, as the only healthy prelude to reconciliation and a new opportunity to keep the promise which in the recent past he had so miserably failed to fulfill?

4.3   Effect

Our understanding of the plot of the story is of no small significance. For the particular plot which the story has will have a great deal to do with the *effect* of the story on the readers or the listeners, whether ancient or modern. Will the readers or the listeners meet in this story a Peter who, on being confronted by Jesus face to face after denying him, had totally forgotten about his disgraceful deed? Or will they meet a Peter whose memory of his last act towards Jesus before his Lord's death burdens him with remorse and shame? If the Peter they meet is the former sort of person, there is a good chance they will feel repelled by him. To forget about an act of such profound negative consequences for his own over-blown image of himself as well as for his relationship with Jesus is almost beyond comprehension. But if in the story the Peter they meet is the latter sort of person, they are likely to be drawn into sympathy with him, even find in him a companion of their own shame in their relationship to Jesus and a means of being reconciled to him and called by him to a life of renewed commitment and service.

4.4   Theology of judgment.

Besides affecting the plot of the story, the response that the readers and listeners may have to Peter, and the consequent meaning and impact the conversation may have on them, the oral interpretation may also have a profound influence on the *theology* of the readers and listeners. First, it ought to affect their theology of *judgment*. What attitude does Jesus display towards Peter's shameful behavior? Is he warm and understanding, as one popular way of reading his words presents him? Does he put aside Peter's failure to be what he promised more readily than Peter put it aside himself? Or does Jesus rather regard Peter's disgraceful deed with utmost seriousness? Does he make him taste the bitter fruit of his sin as the only medicine which can restore his relationship with Jesus to health? Does that bitter fruit consist not only of the name by which Jesus addresses Peter (which reflects Peter's failure to live up to Jesus' assessment of his character and the role to which Jesus called him) and the question which Jesus puts to him, but also in the tone of voice with which Jesus speaks to Peter? In other words, does Jesus' tone of voice soften the impact of the name by which he addresses this weak disciple and the question he puts to him by being warmly reassuring, or does Jesus' attitude contribute to that name a sting? This is a question not only of what readers and listeners will *think* about the significance of the name and the question for Jesus' attitude towards Peter's sin, but of what they will *experience* from his tone of voice in the course of hearing this story. That may have a powerful and lasting impact on their understanding of Jesus' attitude towards their own failures in their relationship with him. Contemporary listeners are usually repelled by a rendering of this story in which Jesus is made to sound distressed and biting in his attitude towards Peter instead of understanding and warm. Such an oral presentation conflicts with their theology of Judgment. The question is, which is more likely to have been the theology of Judgment of the original narrator? What theology of Judgment is his tone of voice likely to have expressed?

4.5   Christology.

4.51   The theology of judgment expressed in the oral interpretation of Jesus' words is bound up with the Fourth Evangelist's *christology*. For Jesus' attitude towards the deeds of others is one aspect of his character.

4.52   Culpepper summarizes his survey of the emotions and motives of Jesus in the Fourth Gospel by saying that Ernst Käsemann's view of John's Jesus "as a god 'striding upon the earth' is not far from the truth" and that "later docetic interpretations of the gospel are not entirely ill-founded" (112–3). Culpepper's statement is indicative of the importance of attitude in the oral interpretation of the words of Jesus for christology. My own analysis of Jesus' emotions and attitudes in the Fourth Gospel leads me to the conclusion that it is misleading at best.

4.53   It is certainly true that throughout the Fourth Gospel Jesus is bold, confident, and in control of what is happening to him. When people make requests of him, he is unaffected by their feelings of urgency (2:3–4; 11:3–7) and even of their perception of their need (11:21, 32). Instead he responds according to a calendar and diagnosis of his own, which results from his constant communion with his Father. To that extent the Jesus of the Fourth Gospel is god-like and does not function like other human beings.

4.54   But if the description of Jesus as god-like in the Fourth Gospel is intended to mean that he is unemotional or that he is uninvolved in human life and unaffected by what people do, that is clearly false. First of all, we have seen that there is a surprising richness in the variety of emotions which are attributed to him, especially given the paucity of explicit references to his feelings. Beyond that the Jesus of the Fourth Gospel is very much concerned with the needs of human beings, even though he is very independent of their influence in making his response to them. His mission was to save the world (3:16 is only the most famous of many statements to this effect). That is his resolute purpose while he walks the earth. We have seen a number of instances, including 21:15–17, in which his words in response to those who are attracted or committed to him suggest that he is feeling a greater or lesser degree of distress when they exhibit inadequate faith or fail him in some way.

4.55   But here is where oral interpretation of Jesus' words play a critical role in the christology of the Fourth Gospel. When, in line with a prevalent current tradition for reading the scriptures, readers consistently endow Jesus' words with an attitude of objective detachment regardless of clues to the contrary, they *impose* on the Gospel a docetic christology which flies in the face of the clues. A Jesus who is personally uninvolved and unaffected by the responses of human beings to him may be the kind of Christ they will know in their own relationship with him. If, on the other hand, readers read the words of Jesus with the feelings suggested by the evidence, they and their listeners will meet a different Jesus in the Fourth Gospel, and their own relationship with Jesus may be transformed.

4.6   A sense of presence.

4.61   Let me return to Kelber's work before I close. The narrative (plot), experiential (effect), theological (theology of judgment and christology) alternatives which I have described above are functions of one aspect of the elocutionary quality of language that is not read silently but heard, namely, the emotional. The elocution of the oral gospel is not discussed by Kelber. In his examination of the oral tradition he focuses his attention more on the mnemonic characteristics of the particular oral stories taken up by Mark, and on the variation that characterizes the handing on of those stories by memory, in the absence of anything so fixed as a written text.

4.62   But there is another characteristic of spoken words that Kelber does emphasize in his description of the oral tradition, which is a direct product of the fact it was heard, and on which I have not yet touched. I quote him (18–19):

> Spoken words breathe life, drawing their strength from sound. They carry a sense of presence, intensity, and instantaneousness that writing fails to convey. "One cannot have voice without presence, at least suggested presence." [Quotation from Walter Ong, *The Presence of the Word*, 114.] Moreover, sounded words emanate from one person and resonate in another, moving along the flow and ebb of human life. They address hearers directly and engage them personally in a manner unat-

tainable by the written medium. One can well imagine Jesus'
words interacting with people and their lives, and enacting presence amidst hearers.

Kelber speaks of this again in his final chapter, where he describes
the way in which writing, a paucity of sayings of Jesus, and the composing
of an historicizing framework with narrative coherence have functioned
together to silence this living voice and bring about Jesus' death. I must
confess that I do not thoroughly grasp Kelber's very complex view in this
chapter. But the quotation above states well the power of the sound of a
living voice to create a sense of presence. I disagree only with his view
that this same sense of presence is excluded by writing as such, or by the
absence of material from the sayings tradition, or by the coherent and
historicizing narrative framework which Mark created.
4.63   Whether or not a sense of presence is excluded by a written text
depends wholly upon the social setting in which the text is used and how
it functions in that setting. In the case of the written Gospels, since they
were read aloud, the sound of the living voice doing the reading was as
capable of mediating a sense of presence as was a voice speaking from
memory.
4.64   Nor is a sense of presence dependent on the presence or absence
of traditional material from the sayings genre. Jesus speaks in stories and
dialogs as well as sayings. A sense of presence can be as vivid when his
words are brief and in response to the words of another as when he
teaches at some length. Matthew, Luke, and John did not revive the voice
of the living Lord by taking up more sayings into their Gospels than Mark
had (Kelber: 208–9). They did so by writing a Gospel that people read
aloud.
4.65   A sense of presence is also not excluded by a narrative framework
such as Mark or John has composed (Kelber: 108). For when the entire
narrative, which does indeed place Jesus in the past, is read aloud, the
events of the past are recreated and become present for the listeners
again, along with them with whom the events are concerned.
5.   Exegesis and current prejudice.
5.1   One more matter remains to be attended to before I bring this essay
to an end. There is in our day a great impediment which prevents the
texts of the Gospels from having the impact on the experience and
theology of the readers and listeners which the clues to the emotional
character of their sound suggests they should. That impediment is a
product of the social setting in which they are used. For among scholars
and in many white American and Northern European churches today,
there is a widespread preference for an aesthetic style which one recent
writer has characterized as

> straightforward, unadorned, unemotional, economical and care-
> fully proportioned. Its purpose is not to inspire emotionally, but
> to bring order out of chaos and make the unknown known. It is
> not an esthetically free and natural style. It is esthetically re-
> strained. Everything is under control. Its value is measured in
> terms of the skill with which this control is maintained. (Pirsig: 61)

When readers of the Biblical narrative bring the oral interpretation of its
words under the sway of this aesthetic style, the characters are restricted
in the emotions they can exhibit. Detachment and objectivity are practically all that is permitted to be in their repertoire, along with occasional
expressions of gentle understanding and, in the reading of the passion
narratives, mild sadness.

5.2   My investigation of the evidence for the original oral interpretation
of Jn 21:15–17 suggests that in the ancient world not only were written
texts read aloud virtually without exception. In addition, a different
aesthetic preference governed the character of that oral reading. Amos
Wilder put it this way:

> when we picture to ourselves the early Christian narrators we
> should make full allowance for animated and expressive narration.
> In ancient times even when one read to oneself from a book, one
> always read aloud. Oral speech also was less inhibited than today.
> It is suggestive that in teaching the rabbis besides using cantilla-
> tion also used 'didactic facial expression,' as well as 'gestures and
> bodily movements to impart dramatic shape to the doctrinal
> material.' When we think of the early church meetings and
> testimonies and narrations we are probably well guided if we
> think of the way in which Vachel Lindsay read or of the appropri-
> ate readings of James Weldon Johnson's God's Trombones. (64.
> Quotations are from Gerhardsson, *Memory and Manuscript*, 168.)

6.   Postscript

Like a review of a recent musical performance, this essay ought to be
read in the context of hearing the oral renditions of the narrative with
which it is concerned. As a contribution to that context, a cassette tape of
my oral interpretation of the narratives concerning Peter in the Fourth
Gospel is available at the cost of $2.00. Please send your request to me at
Lancaster Theological Seminary, 555 West James Street, Lancaster, PA
17603.

NOTES

[1]My colleague David Hopkins points out that Hebrew narrative is reticient in regard to
emotion. But that is true only in regard to explicit verbal content. See Gunkel: 62: "But even

when the story-teller said nothing of the soul-life of his heroes, his hearer did not entirely fail to catch an impression of it. We must recall . . . that we are dealing with orally recited stories. Between narrator and hearer there is another link than that of words; the tone of voice talks, the expression of the face or the gestures of the narrator. Joy and grief, love, anger, jealousy, hatred, emotion, and all the other moods of his heroes, shared by the narrator, were thus imparted to his hearers without the utterance of a word."

[2] Kelber seems to know that Mark was read aloud. On p. 209, for example, he speaks of the "hearer of the Markan gospel." But apparently he has not seen the implications of that fact.

[3] "The text . . . has brought about a freezing of oral life into textual still life." (91)

[4] ". . . hearers or readers are excluded from the process of composition." (92)

[5] It is not necessary for my purposes to make a textual decision in regard to *probaton* and *probation*. See Brown: 1105, for a clear presentation of the alternatives.

[6] The significance of the use of these two different verbs is greatly debated. I shall discuss this problem, because these verbs are central to Jesus' questions and Peter's answers, and are therefore of great importance for the movement of the conversation. There is also disagreement over the significance of the other variations (see Brown: 1104–5). But I shall not discuss them, because they are not of crucial importance for the movement.

[7] For this survey I lean heavily on Brown. See 497–9, 1102–3 for a full discussion.

[8] Cf. Lindars: 634–5: "There may be no distinction of meaning, but the variation may be intended to allow a wider range of literary allusion." He goes on to relate 21:15ff to Peter's promise in 13:37 and to 15:13.

[9] Are all these verses, from chapters 10, 12, 13, 15, and 18, which I have used in interpreting 21:15–19, from the hand of the Evangelist, while 21:15–19 itself is from the hand of a Redactor? Yes! How, then, can we draw on these earlier passages to interpret the Redactor's work? By making the reasonable assumption that the Redactor is not just tacking new stories onto the end of the Evangelist's work but is consciously building on it. Cf. R. Schnackenburg, 1982: 362. Note also, in contrast to Schnackenburg, the possibility that the *Redactor* (not the Evangelist) has omitted from the Evangelist's story of the denial (Jn 18:15–18, 25–27) a brief report that Peter remembered Jesus' prophecy of the denial and wept (cf. Mk 14:72), and that he expanded it into the dramatic dialog which we number 21:15–19. B. Lindars and R. Brown think that the Evangelist may have omitted details from his tradition and expanded those details into a new narrative unit (see Brown: 997). So the Redactor may here be employing the same approach to the tradition available to him.

[10] In the Fourth Gospel *lypeō* connotes intense emotion. In 16:20–22 *lypeō* and *lypē* are used for the emotion of the disciples at Jesus' departure through death; are parallel to two verbs used elsewhere of those who are lamenting at a death, *klaiō* (Jn 11:31, 33) and *thrēneō* (Lk 23:27); are connected with the *thlipsis* of a woman giving birth to a child; and are contrasted to *chairō* and *chara*.

[11] This manner of orally interpreting the Bible is often advocated for all texts, in total disregard for the question whether it is exegetically justified. See for example Bonhoeffer: 55–6: "How shall we read the Scriptures? . . . The more artless, the more objective, the more humble one's attitude toward the material is, the better will the reading accord with the subject." The reasons Bonhoeffer offers for this manner of reading I find to be most confusing and in need of a lengthy analysis which would not be appropriate in this essay. But I myself have often heard it argued that an objective reading should be practiced because it is *interpretively neutral*. It leaves the listeners free, it is said, to come to their own interpretations of the texts. I would counter this claim with the observation that many years of objective oral reading in churches has simply not had this result. It has not fostered a freedom to interpret in many different ways. Rather it has fostered a prejudice for an objective oral reading in listeners and a prejudice against other ways of reading and hearing it. Freedom of interpretation and of exegetical exploration is more likely to arise from hearing many different oral renditions, not just an objective one.

[12] Any of these attitudes can be adopted in speaking the first answer of Peter, regardless of the translation being read.

[13] Cf. Marsh: 669. His distinction between the translation of *agapaō* and *phileō* leads him to the view that "Peter, who would on some occasions undoubtedly have answered with a confident 'Yes,' now knows that he can make no such claim." Thus, when Jesus asks Peter whether he "loves" him, in the sense of divinely conditioned loyalty, Peter affirms his "love" only in the sense of human care. I do not believe this distinction between *agapaō* and *phileō* is correct. Thus I would argue that Peter is claiming no less a love than Jesus is asking about. But in claiming to have that love for Jesus, Peter is well aware that his previous actions made it appear quite otherwise.

[14] The variant reading *Iōna* for *Iōannou* found in some manuscripts is probably due to assimilation to Bar Jonah in Mt 16:17 (Brown: 76).

[15] In 1:42 Jesus calls him "*Simon, ho huios Iōannou*;" in 21:15–7, "*Simōn Iōannou.*" In the later formulation, the words *ho huios* are to be understood (Robertson: 501).

[16] The situation is similar in regard to the giving of the name Israel to Jacob at Gen 32:28 (*klēthēsetai to onoma sou*). Before 32:28 the name Israel is not used, and after that verse it is used both by the narrator and in direct speech (49:2, where Jacob/Israel himself says, "Listen to Israel your father"). The difference is that after that point the name Jacob continues to be used as well as the name Israel.

[17] The verb *emblepsas*, they observe, indicates Jesus' insight into Peter's character (Brown: 74; Lindars: 115; Barrett: 152; Bultmann, 1971: 102; Schnackenburg, 1968: 310–11).

[18] Cf. Lindars: 116: "John here makes it [the nickname] the result of Jesus' estimate of Simon's character"; Brown: 80: "As is known from the OT, the giving of a new name has a direct relation to the role the man so designated will play in salvation history (Gen xvii 5, xxxii 28). On this point Matthew's account is more polished than John's for Matthew explains the relation of the new name ('rock') to Peter's role as the foundation stone of the Church. John stresses only that the name came from Jesus' insight into Simon ('Jesus looked at him')"; Barrett: 152: "Jesus knows at once the character and destiny of Peter"; Schnackenburg, 1968: 311: "he 'looks at' Simon and knows all about him, and at the same time reveals what his future name will be."

[19] Zahn: 695: ". . . especially emphatic reminder of that which this disciple is in origin, in contrast to that to which Jesus had called him and what he wanted to make out of him" (quoted in Schnackenburg, 1982: 481, n. 55).

[20] Cf. above, pars. 3.132–4, my rejection of the view that *phileō* denotes a stronger love than *agapaō*.

[21] Culpepper: 110: "His 'dig' at Nicodemus (3:10) shows a touch of sarcasm. . . ."

WORKS CONSULTED

Augustine
    1960   *The Confessions of St. Augustine.* Trans., with an introduction and notes by John K. Ryan. Garden City: Doubleday.

Barrett, C. K.
    1955   *The Gospel according to St. John: An Introduction with Commentary and Notes on the Greek Text.* London: SPCK.

Bauer, Walter
    1979   *A Greek-English Lexicon of the New Testament and Other Early Christian Literature.* Trans. and adaptation by William F. Arndt and F. Wilbur Gingrich. 2d ed. Revised and Augmented by F. Wilbur Gingrich and Frederick W. Danker. Chicago: The University of Chicago Press.

Bernard, J. H.

    1928   *A Critical and Exegetical Commentary on the Gospel according to St. John.* Vol. II. Ed. A.. H. McNeile. The International Critical Commentary. Edinburgh: T. & T. Clark.

Blass, F. and A. Debrunner

    1961   *A Greek Grammar of the New Testament and Other Early Christian Literature.* Trans. and rev. by Robert W. Funk. Chicago: The University of Chicago Press.

Bonhoeffer, Dietrich

    1954   *Life Together.* Trans., and with an Introduction by John W. Doberstein. New York: Harper & Row.

Brown, Raymond E.

    1966,   *The Gospel according to John.* Anchor Bible. Vols. 29 and 29A.
    1970   Garden City: Doubleday.

Bultmann, Rudolf

    1964   *"anaginōskō, anagnōsis," Theological Dictionary of the New Testament.* Vol. I. Ed. Gerhard Kittel. Trans. and ed. by Geoffrey W. Bromiley. Grand Rapids: Wm. B. Eerdmans. Pp. 343–4.

    1971   *The Gospel of John: A Commentary.* Transl by G. R. Beasley-Murray, et al. Philadelphia: Westminster.

Culpepper, R. Alan

    1983   *Anatomy of the Fourth Gospel: A Study in Literary Design.* Philadelphia: Fortress.

Gunkel, Hermann

    1964   *The Legends of Genesis: The Biblical Saga and History.* Trans. by W. H. Carruth. New York: Shocken.

Haenchen, Ernst

    1971   *The Acts of the Apostles.* Trans. by Bernard Noble and Gerald Shinn, under the supervision of Hugh Anderson, revised and brought up to date by R. McL. Wilson. Philadelphia: Westminster.

Hoskyns, Edwyn C.

    1947   *The Fourth Gospel.* Ed. Francis Noel Davey. 2d ed. London: Faber & Faber.

JB

    1968   *The Jerusalem Bible: New Testament.* Garden City: Doubleday.

Kelber, Werner

    1983   *The Oral and the Written Gospel: The Hermeneutics of Speaking and Writing in the Synoptic Tradition, Mark, Paul, and Q.* Philadelphia: Fortress.

Lindars, Barnabas
    1972   *The Gospel of John*. New Century Bible. London: Oliphants.

Marrou, H. I.
    1956   *A History of Education in Antiquity*. Trans. by George Lamb. New York: Sheed and Ward.

Marsh, John
    1968   *The Gospel of St. John*. The Pelican New Testament Commentaries. Harmondsworth: Penguin.

Moulton, James H.
    1908   *A Grammar of New Testament Greek*. Vol. I: *Prolegomena*. 3d ed. Edinburgh: T. & T. Clark.

NEB
    1970   *The New English Bible New Testament*. Oxford: Oxford University Press.

Parish, Wayland Maxfield
    1966   *Reading Aloud*. 4th ed. New York: Ronald Press.

Phillips, J. B.
    1959   *The New Testament in Modern English*. Trans. by J. B. Phillips. New York: Macmillan.

Pirsig, Robert M.
    1974   *Zen and the Art of Motorcycle Maintenance: An Inquiry into Values*. New York: Bantam.

Robertson, A. T.
    1934   *A Grammar of the Greek New Testament in the Light of Historical Research*. Nashville: Broadman.

RSV
    1971   *Revised Standard Version of the Bible*. New Testament Section, 2d ed. Division of Christian Education of the National Council of the Churches of Christ in the United States of America.

Schnackenburg, Rudolf
    1968   *The Gospel according to St. John: Introduction and Commentary on Chapters 1–4*. Herder's Theological Commentary on the New Testament. Vol. I. Trans. by Kevin Smyth. New York: Herder and Herder.
    1982   *The Gospel according to St. John: Commentary on Chapters 13–21*. Vol. III. Trans. by David Smith and G. A. Kon. New York: Crossroad.

Widengren, Geo.
    1959   "Oral Tradition and Written Literature," *Acta Orientalia* 23: 201–262.

Wilder, Amos
    1964   *The Language of the Gospel: Early Christian Rhetoric*. New York: Harper & Row.

BIBLICAL HERMENEUTICS AND THE ANCIENT ART OF COMMUNICATION: A RESPONSE

Werner H. Kelber

Rice University

Spoken language is the substratum of everything human and divine that transpires in the Bible . . .

Robert Alter, *The Art of Biblical Narrative*

. . . hermeneutics traditionally has been concerned not with language *per se* but with the language of texts. What, then, is the relationship between the hermeneutical appropriation of texts and the hermeneutics of discourse as language's own self-presentation?

Carl A. Raschke, *The Alchemy of the Word: Language and the End of Theology*

0. Broadly conceived, the present issue of *Semeia* seeks to bring to the attention of biblical scholars some aspects of current work on oral verbalization and the technology of writing. Thriving in a virtually boundless interdisciplinary ecumenicity, orality-literacy studies presently engage more than ninety language areas. Since 1960 more than 1,000 books and articles on matters of speech and writing have appeared in fields as diverse as Slavica, Arabic studies, Judaica, Vedic Sanscrit, Old English, French, Spanish and German, a host of African traditions, classics, philosophy, medieval studies, comparative literature, linguistics, folklore studies, and so forth. In 1986 the University of Missouri-Columbia in cooperation with Slavica Press of Ohio State University began publication of ORAL TRADITION, a triannual journal dedicated to the field of research and scholarship on oral tradition and literature. Its editor, John Miles Foley, himself a prolific scholar of oral language and theory, had earlier completed a comprehensive annotated bibliography on *Oral-*

Formulaic Theory and Research (1985) for which he also wrote a highly informative introduction. The vitality of orality-literacy studies is further confirmed by the fact that a new journal, CULTURAL AN-THROPOLOGY, edited by George Marcus, chairman of the anthropology Department at Rice University, has assigned its entire second issue (May, 1986) to matters of speech and writing.

0.1 Specifically, the four preceding essays address my recent book, *The Oral and the Written Gospel* (1983; henceforth *OWG*) in which I sought to broaden biblical hermeneutics by reconsidering speech and writing in early Christianity. It was, of course, the assigned business of form criticism to come to terms with speech and oral tradition. But, as I tried to show, the form critics embarked upon their project with a pittance of linguistic reflection. By definition, the new discipline clung to the analysis of *form*, which is itself a visually grounded concept. Concern for a spatial, architectural vision of language, rather than for acoustic, rhythmic principles of verbalization, precluded the development of a conceptual apparatus commensurate with spoken words. Moreover, form criticism's search for the "original" form arose out of literate presuppositions, as did its preoccupation with transmissional processes. The resultant paradigm of the tradition reflected deeply ingrained habits of seeing words develop in a thoroughly sequential fashion. When Bultmann categorically disavowed a differentiated treatment of speech versus text (1970: 91 [1963: 87]), form criticism had almost from its inception aborted its principal objective. Today we face the anomalous situation of a thriving oral research in many branches of the humanities which has escaped most students of the Bible, further contributing to the isolation of biblical scholarship from humanistic studies in general.

1.0 The difficulty most biblical scholars encounter in conceptualizing speech is related to our predominantly text-bound culture and training. In a sense literacy took itself to be normative with the canonization of Scripture. Protestantism in particular enforced the power of the written word, whereas Catholicism viewed Scripture as on a par with the "unwritten traditions." Under the powerful impact of typographic pressures, however, biblical scholarship has become synonymous with textual scholarship. Laden down with centuries of interiorized scriptural modes and modern literary habits, we are conditioned to discover intelligence in literate terms. The text has gripped our imagination to a degree that it is accepted as the principal instrument of religious, civilized existence. Yet Arnoldo Momigliano's perceptive query "whether anyone ever became a Jewish proselyte *because* he read the Bible" (1981: 332) applies with equal strength to early Christian converts. Speech was the medium of proclamation. In antiquity, listening audiences by far prevailed over reading individuals. In Christian antiquity, the oral proclamation of the gospel was the rule. And yet, speech has not been given the place it deserves in our reconstruction of early Christianity. We tend to see the latter as a history dominated by the ubiquity of texts.

1.1   Perhaps our greatest difficulty in understanding speech lies with its insubstantial, ephemeral quality which is "entirely uncontainable and incomprehensible according to formal, linear, or analytic models" (Bruns, 1982: 96). Indeed, how can one conceptualize the traveling of speech by word of mouth, namely oral tradition/composition itself? We cannot really imagine words spoken at one place, then spoken by the same person at another place, and again resumed by others who heard the speaker, except via the paradigm of rectilinear transmission. But the pipeline model has as little meaning in oral communication as do the categories of authentic versus secondary speech. Here as elsewhere science may provide us with a helpful model. In quantum systems such as atoms an electron can "jump" from one state to another without actually occupying an intermediate position. Such is the behavior of oral communication. It consists of discreet acts of speech, separated by intervals of non-speaking, and unconnectable by temporal or spatial tracts.

2.0   In chapter 4 of OWG I described Paul as an oral traditionalist. What deserves to be pointed out in this connection is that biblical scholars are beginning to sense the signal importance of rhetoric for Pauline studies. Although rhetoric as a subject taught in ancient schools and reflected on in text books could come into existence only with the help of script, it is at bottom oral rather than textual, and practical more than philosophical. Theologians of the stature of Ambrose, Jerome, Chrysostom, Augustine, and Methodius, among many others, could well appreciate the Pauline letters as rhetorical pieces because these men were rhetorically trained and practicing rhetoricians themselves. They still lived in a world in which rhetoric was a most serious and consequential activity. We who live in a culture in which the words "rhetoric" and "rhetorical" are almost always used pejoratively, must relearn what for the ancients was a fact of life.

2.1   Hans D. Betz (1975; 1979) and Wilhelm Wuellner (1976; 1977; 1978) share the distinction of having taken a lead in reforming our habits of reading Paul's letters. They have introduced us into the topological and forensic style of Pauline rhetoric, thereby loosening our dependence on the literary logic of systematic progression. The apostle's letters, we now begin to grasp, grew out of the disputatious climate of antiquity where opinions were often communicated against opposition. Digression and sudden shifts in presentation frequently turn out to be conventional devices for affecting hearers. Argumentative schemata and conventional *topoi* are meant to alter convictions, to heighten a sense of communion, to commit hearers to values, to elicit actions, or to discourage certain practices. Insofar as recent commentaries such as Hans Conzelmann's *1 Corinthians* (1975) or Ernst Kaesemann's *Romans* (1980) give priority to theological ideas while treating matters of style, discourse, and rhetoric as more or less incidental, they still betray the idealistic legacy of modern biblical studies. The development from rhetoric to logic, including a formalized theological logic, took centuries of evolution in human consciousness (Ong, 1982: 139–205). Paul is on the whole committed more to religious persuasion by oratory, than to purely intellectualized theology.

3.0   In turning to my work on Mark and the synoptic tradition, I shall address the principal point made by both Bommershine and Bartholomew that the gospel was intended to be heard rather than read in isolation. In their view, I have telescoped 1800 years of writing and reading habits upon the text, failing to appreciate its oral functioning.

3.1   A major concern of chapters 1, 2, 3 and 5 of OWG was to reconsider the gospel's relation to antecedent tradition. Whereas the classic paradigm was (and largely remains) one of thoroughgoing stability, I sought to demonstrate both Mark's indebtedness to and distanciation from oral materials and values. I granted the existence of textuality in the synoptic tradition (OWG: 23, 91), but stressed the presence of a predominantly oral state of mind. Mark, I suggested, went against basic oral impulses when he kept sayings at a minimum, displaced the crucial oral authorities of tradition (disciples, family, prophets), and silenced the voice of the risen Lord while refocusing upon the earthly Jesus and his death. As Ong has emphasized in his essay, and as I reinforced in my contribution to this issue, Mark's text constitutes interpretation. Together with James M. Robinson (1970; 1982) and M. Eugene Boring (1977; 1982) I see canonical Mark as a rather radical revision of the genre of the sayings gospel. Dominic Crossan has strongly supported the revisionist identity of Mark, although he sees a far more complex picture of the kind of traditions Mark revises (1985). This interpretive, revisionist view of Mark challenges not only Bultmann and Gerhardsson, but also recent work by Rudolf Pesch (1976; 1977), Martin Hengel (1983: 221–65), and Rainer Riesner (1984), all of whom accentuate stability and continuity on the matter of tradition and gospel.

3.2   In order to guard against an exaggerated notion of Markan textuality I asked both Albert Lord and John Foley whether they had ever in their research of oral traditions encountered a story narrating a hero's full career from birth to death. The answer I received from both scholars was a negative one. The important lesson to be learned from this is that the written gospel cannot very likely be considered directly transcribed primary orality. While I have repeatedly stressed the oral functioning of the narrative gospel (OWG: 94, 209, 217), I would suggest that Mark, by synthesizing, composing, and revising traditions, accomplished a narrative that in this form his ancient hearers never heard before. Literacy did make a difference in this case. On the other hand, I tend not to agree with scholars who have approached the gospel with categories derived from 19th and 20th century literature and literary theories. The 19th century novel in particular has internalized in most of us narrative expectations that are quite alien to writers and hearers of the first century gospel. I take, therefore, a position midway between those who view the gospel as a fully plotted, deeply psychological narrative, and others who hear it as a virtually unedited rendition of oral composition. The gospel, as I perceive it, is at once more thoroughly entrenched in oral strategies and verbalization than our modern literary aesthetics will let us know and more informed by literary rationality than the thesis of oral composition would allow. As the eye begins to share responsibilities with the ear, linearity seeks compositional control over the episodic arrangement. This tension between the oral and the written is by no means an uncommon sight in the ancient art of communication.[1]

3.3 Is it admissible to argue, as I did repeatedly in OWG, that the gospel's text brings about an eclipse of voice? Boomershine and Bartholomew consider the proposal incompatible with the hearer-friendly nature of the text. Obviously, no text has it in its power to put an end to speech (OWG: 93). But if we conceive of Mark's function not as primarily preservative, fortifying memory against forgetfulness, but as primarily interpretive, redirecting a course of tradition, do we not have to acknowledge the gospel as a new synthesis? If, in other words, oral lore is recontextualized, is it not in a sense muted and taken away from speakers and hearers? Of course, the gospel enters into a social contract of its own. Boomershine and Bartholomew are quite correct in suggesting in effect that we have emphasized the cognitive significance of gospel texts at the neglect of their affective and acoustic quality. I sought to do justice to the communicative nature of the written gospel by interpreting it as parable which in its openendedness leaves the narrative outcome up to hearers/readers. To be sure, a full-scale hearer-responsive or reader-responsive analysis deserves a book-length treatment in its own right.

3.4 Lest we think the discovery of the gospels as sound-conscious discourse will return us to a primal state of story-telling, we need perennially reminding of our hermeneutical condition. The gospels as texts can and do in fact enjoy the stability of documented existence denied to oral speech. By the same token, the written gospels do not accommodate to changing circumstances and to different audiences as oral proclamation does. Texts fossilize. For this and for many other reasons Mark's gospel, itself an interpretation, inevitably confronts us with the task of interpretation.

4.0 The discipleship narration, as is well known, has long been a bone of contention in Markan studies. Boomershine selects it as a prime example of my misguided reading of the gospel. The issue comes down to the question of how hearers/readers are expected to identify with the disciples. Boomershine finds discipleship narrated according to the rhythm of negative norms followed by sympathetic distance, without ever fully estranging hearers from the disciples. I see the overall pattern as one of positivity (especially in the call, the appointment, and the placement of the Twelve into the inside circle) followed by increasing negativity. While positive features decline, negative directives intensify, alienating hearers/readers from the disciples. I do not disagree with Boomershine that sympathies for the disciples and for Peter are aroused, although I find his examples of the Transfiguration and of Gethsemane not nearly as convincing as the case of Peter's Denial. The weeping Peter (Mk 14:72) does indeed elicit sympathies and pity. But is it sympathy for one who will eventually be restored, or pity because one senses the narrative fulfilment of Jesus' words of discipleship: "For whoever wishes to save his life shall lose it . . . For whoever is ashamed of Me and My words . . . the Son of Man will also be ashamed of . . ." (Mk 8:35, 38)?

4.1   In my view, the precise definition of the narrative pattern of Markan discipleship is role reversal: the insiders are turned into outsiders. Only in Mark are the outsider characteristics (Mk 4:11-12) applied to the disciples (Mk 8:17-18). And only in Mark does the "hina doctrine of narrative" (Kermode, 1979: 33) anticipate the uncompromising exclusion of outsiders: "Those who are on the outside get everything in parables, so that (hina) seeing they may see and not perceive, and hearing they may hear and not understand, lest (mēpote) they return again and be forgiven" (Mk 4: 11-12). Boomershine also suggests that my interpretation of Markan discipleship is historically improbable. Yet rather than adjusting Mark to what we think early Christian history must have been like, I take the astounding oddness of the written gospel as a challenge to conventional modes of thought. In turning to Havelock's reading of Plato's repudiation of the poets (OWG: 95-98) I did not wish to suggest a direct historical analogy between Plato's situation and the Markan one. Least of all did I intend to transform the evangelist into a first century Plato. What I found in Havelock's masterful treatment of Plato was the kind of heuristic model that for the first time helped me understand the evangelist's drive to loosen our dependence on his oral precursors.

5.0   Farrell has questioned my christological assessment of the suffering Jesus (Mk 14-16) as the antihero (OWG: 197). This definition was based on the contrast I discern between the orally based heroic and polarization stories and the textually grounded passion narrative. Proceeding from Ong's observation that heroic figures tend to decline with writing (1967: 205), I assumed a narrative christology that guided hearers/readers from the hero to the antihero. But it may be more in keeping with Markan christology to understand the cross as the redefinition of heroism. Seen in this light, the gospel may be said to undertake a transformation of an orally based christology. The new christology of heroism, richly feeding on Scripture and thoroughly ironic in impact, reaches its culmination in the passion narrative.

6.0   There is lastly the issue of presence and absence. Bartholomew wonders why I denied the written gospel the kind of presence I acknowledged for the oral gospel. As I pointed out repeatedly in *OWG*, the vocal communication of the gospel created a powerful sense of the presence of Christ. The sayings gospel, while committed to writing, retained the thrust of the oral kerygma by upholding the authority of the living Lord. The Proclaimer continued to be the Proclaimer. It is against this background of the powers of the oral proclamation that one can appreciate Crossan's definition of Mark as a "form for absence" (1978: 41; *OWG*: 210). The absence of a resurrection appearance story in the written gospel is hardly a trifling matter. Whatever else Mark may have wished to communicate, the presence of the living Lord was not his chief kerygmatic objective. On this issue of presence and absence, as well as on other matters of biblical hermeneutics and theology, biblical scholars ought to reflect deeply on the grammatological philosophy of Jacques Derrida (1976; Schneidau, 1982: 5–27). He does, of course, wish to purge the notion of presence from our thinking altogether, and he has never acknowledged familiarity with the work on orality by Havelock, Lord, Ong, and others. But at the very least he can serve as a necessary antidote to a theologically indiscriminate invocation of presence[2]. And so can Mark.

NOTES

[1]Eric A. Havelock, "The Alphabetization of Homer," in *The Literate Revolution in Greece and Its Cultural Consequences* (Princeton, N.J.: Princeton University Press, 1982), 182: "The works of Greek literature after the Homeric transcription occurred are composed in an increasing tension between the genius of oral and the genius of written composition."

[2]On Derrida and the issue of presence and absence in the fourth gospel, see my forthcoming article in *Oral Tradition* (1987): "The Logos and the Logoi in the Fourth Gospel: Charismatic Speech, Narrative Text, Logocentric Metaphysics."

WORKS CONSULTED

Alter, Robert
   1981   *The Art of Biblical Narrative*. New York: Basic Books.
Betz, Hans Dieter
   1975   "The Literary Composition and Function of Paul's Letter to the Galatians." *NTS* 21: 353–79.
   1979   *Galatians. A Commentary on Paul's Letter to the Churches in Galatia*. Philadelphia, PA: Fortress Press.

Boring, M. Eugene
    1977   "The Paucity of Sayings in Mark: A Hypothesis." Pp. 371–77 in
             SBL Seminar Papers. Missoula, MT: Scholars Press.
    1982   *Sayings of the Risen Jesus. Christian Prophecy in the Synoptic
             Tradition. SNTS MS* 46. Cambridge: Cambridge University
             Press.

Bruns, Gerald L.
    1982   *Inventions. Writing, Textuality, and Understanding in Literary
             History*. New Haven and London: Yale University Press.

Bultmann, Rudolf
    1970   *Die Geschichte der Synoptischen Tradition. FRLANT* 29, *NF* 12.
             8th ed. Göttingen: Vandenhoeck & Ruprecht [Eng. trans., *The
             History of the Synoptic Tradition*. New York: Harper & Row,
             1963].

Conzelmann, Hans
    1975   *1 Corinthians*. Eng. trans. by James W. Leitch. Philadelphia,
             PA: Fortress Press.

Crossan, John Dominic
    1978   "A Form for Absence: The Markan Creation of Gospel." *Semeia*
             12: 41–55.

Derrida, Jacques
    1976   *Of Grammatology*. Eng. trans. by Gayatri Chakravorty Spivak.
             Baltimore and London: Johns Hopkins University Press.

Foley, John Miles
    1985   *Oral-Formulaic Theory and Research. An Introduction and An-
             notated Bibliography*. Garland Folklore Bibliographies, 6.
             Garland Reference Library of the Humanities, 400, Garland
             Publications.

Havelock, Eric A.
    1982   *The Literate Revolution in Greece and Its Cultural Con-
             sequences*. Princeton, N.J.: Princeton University Press.

Hengel, Martin
    1983   "Probleme des Markusevangeliums." Pp. 221–65 in *Das Evan-
             gelium und die Evangelien*, ed. Peter Stuhlmacher. Tübingen:
             J. C. B. Mohr (Paul Siebeck).

Ernst Kaesemann
    1980   *Commentary on Romans*. Eng. trans. by Geoffrey Bromiley.
             Grand Rapids, MI: Eerdmanns.

Kelber, Werner H.
    1983   *The Oral and the Written Gospel. The Hermeneutics of Speaking
             and Writing in the Synoptic Tradition, Mark, Paul, and Q*.
             Philadelphia, PA: Fortress Press.

Kermode, Frank
    1979   *The Genesis of Secrecy. On the Interpretation of Narrative.*
               Cambridge, MA and London: Harvard University Press.

Momigliano, A. D.
    1981   "Greek Culture and the Jews," in *The Legacy of Greece: A New Appraisal.* Ed. by M. I. Finley. Oxford: Clarendon Press.

Ong, Walter J., S. J.
    1967   *The Presence of the Word. Some Prolegomena for Cultural and Religious History.* New Haven, CT and London: Yale University Press. Paperback ed., Minneapolis, MN: University of Minnesota Press.
    1982   *Introduction* (pp. 139–205) to "A Fuller Course in the Art of Logic Conformed to the Method of Peter Ramus" by John Milton, in *Completed Prose Works of John Milton*, Vol. VIII. New Haven and London: Yale University Press.

Pesch, Rudolf
    1976;   *Das Markusevangelium.* Vol. I, II. Freiburg, Basel, Vienna:
    1977   Herder.

Raschke, Carl A.
    1979   *The Alchemy of the Word. Language and the End of Theology. AAR SR 20.* Missoula, MT: Scholars Press.

Riesner, Rainer
    1984   *Jesus als Lehrer. Eine Untersuchung zum Ursprung der Evangelien-Überlieferung.* 2n ed. *WUNT,* 2nd Reihe 7. Tübingen: J. C. B. Mohr (Paul Siebeck).

Robinson, James M.
    1970   "On the Gattung of Mark (and John)." Pp. 99–129 in *Jesus and Man's Hope*, Vol. I. Pittsburgh, PA: Pittsburgh Theological Seminary.
    1982   "Jesus: From Easter to Valentinus (or to the Apostles' Creed)." *JBL* 101: 5–37.

Schneidau, Herbert N.
    1982   "The Word against the Word: Derrida on Textuality." *Semeia* 23: 5–28.

Wuellner, Wilhelm H.
    1976   "Paul's rhetoric of argumentation in Romans." *CBQ* 38: 330–51.
    1977   "Paul's Rhetoric of Argumentation in Romans: An Alternative to the Donfried-Karris Debate over Romans," in *The Romans Debate*, ed. Karl P. Donfried. Minneapolis, MN: Augsburg.
    1978   "Toposforschung und Torahinterpretation bei Paulus und Jesus." *NTS* 24: 463–83.

NARRATIVE AS INTERPRETATION AND INTERPRETATION OF NARRATIVE: HERMENEUTICAL REFLECTIONS ON THE GOSPELS

Werner H. Kelber
Rice University

ABSTRACT

This essay promotes a general theory of interpretation which seeks to advance hermeneutical reflection on the gospels.

A first part investigates the hermeneutical status of Mark's narrative composition in the context of early Christian traditions. When attention is paid to orality-literacy dynamics, the gospel narrative discloses tension with the genre of sayings or dialogue gospel. The exposition of the narrative gospel as radical interpretation of antecedent tradition raises the issue of revisionism which is held to be of signal importance for biblical hermeneutics.

A second part reflects on the hermeneutical presuppositions of literary criticism with reference to gospel narrativity. When attention is paid to oral, scribal, and typographical dynamics, literary criticism—especially in its formalist, hermetic sense—shows itself to be the child of typographic consciousness. Synoptic scribality, far from positing narrative as a closed world, works out of tradition and in response to audience.

A third part seeks to draw connections between the first century gospel narrator and the twentieth century interpreters of gospel narratives. Inasmuch as the gospel constitutes interpretation itself, readers and scholars who interpret the gospels continue hermeneutical practices pursued by the evangelists and set into motion by others before them. The encompassing condition that unites hearers, readers and exegetes with the evangelists is interpretation.

Alles Verstehen ist Auslegung.

Gadamer, *Wahrheit und Methode*

> Until then I thought each book speaks of the things, human and divine, that lie outside of books. Now I realized that not infrequently books speak of books.
>
> Eco, *The Name of the Rose*

> That is why in so many textual distortions we may count on finding the suppressed and abnegated material hidden away somewhere, though in an altered shape and torn out of its original connection. Only it is not always easy to recognize it.
>
> Freud, *Moses and Monotheism*

> Genetic considerations are not always irrelevant, however, and it is not always a fallacy to discuss achievement and process simultaneously.
>
> Hoy, *The Critical Circle*

> There is a genuine continuity between the operations performed on their material by the evangelists, and the work of the exegetes who, for almost two millennia, have continued their labors.
>
> Kermode, *The Genesis of Secrecy*

0.   The art of telling stories has faithfully accompanied the human race from preliterate to post-modern times. So "natural" appears to be the impulse to narrate that one is hard put to imagine a language or culture devoid of narrative elements. The need to make scraps of life cohere in the imagination and to plot events so as to give them a semblance of coherence and sequentiality may thus reasonably be counted among the human universals. Roland Barthes was of the opinion that narrative "is simply there like life itself . . . international, transhistorical, transcultural" (1977: 77). Hayden White to whom we owe some of the most profound studies on the subject (1973; 1978) viewed narrative as "a panglobal fact of culture" (1980: 5). One may well claim, therefore, that "narrative and narration are less problems than simply data" (White, 1980: 5). It is, however, precisely that which we take most for granted and without which we seem least able to exist that tends to elude our full attention. The very ubiquity of narrative subtly distracts us from according critical recognition to our narrative impulses and performances. We need reminding that narrative, while there like life itself, is not itself life. "No one and nothing *lives* as story" (White, 1978: 111). For life, after all, does not narrate, and narrative is always artificial. Perhaps the impulse to narrate is not quite as "natural" as it seems.

0.1   In the context of ancient literary history, the canonical gospels can hardly claim uniqueness as far as narrativity is concerned. The golden age of Hebrew narrative extended roughly from the tenth to the seventh century B.C.E. Prose narratives, especially in the form of biographies, were a standard feature of Hellenistic culture. In part at least they owed their existence to the desire to keep alive the memory of extraordinary deeds and powers that were associated with famous poets, philosophers, and rulers. It is entirely reasonable, therefore, to examine the gospels by analogy with Greco-Roman forms of narrative (Votaw: 1970; Talbert: 1977; Robbins: 1984). But it remains questionable whether the gospels are fully assimilable to, and explicable by, Hellenistic narrative models, if only because the narration of a crucified Son of God was a moral, aesthetic, and literary monstrosity, contradicting Jewish, Hellenistic, Roman, and barbarian sensibilities (Hengel: 1977). Appeal to Hellenistic biographies will not entirely explain the impulse to narrate the gospel stories. One may also remember that narrative was far from being a uniform mode of expression in the early Christian tradition. Substantial parts of the canon suggest that a faithful commitment to the Christ did not perforce require narrativity. Moreover, a segment of non-canonical Christianity, as will be shown, appears to have been less than friendly toward narrative syntax. It would follow, on this view, that the non-narrative and the anti-narrative tradition in early Christianity itself does not allow us to take the narrative gospel for granted.

0.2   Literary critics have been far from generous in recording the gospels' contribution to Western culture. The monumental research compiled by H. Munro and N. Kershaw Chadwick on nearly 2,400 pages of *The Growth of Literature* (1932–1940), for example, makes only incidental reference to the gospel stories. In what has justly been called a classic, Robert Scholes' and Robert Kellogg's *The Nature of Narrative* (1966), the history of narrative is traced from its oral beginnings to the heights of the nineteenth and twentieth century realistic novel without according the gospels a place in it. Nor are the gospels mentioned in a recent study of the post-classical, Hellenistic birth of the novel, Thomas Hägg's *The Novel in Antiquity* (1983), which examines *inter alia* Philostratus' *Life of Apollonius,* the Alexander Romances, the apocryphal *Acts of the Apostles,* the Pseudo-Clementines, and various hagiographical materials. The critics' reticence to assess the gospels' significance in literary history is all the more puzzling in that these ancient Christian stories continue to occupy a commanding position in Western culture. With the exception of the ancient Hebrew narratives, the gospels are to this day read and recited more than any other single story composed in antiquity. Does overfamiliarity prevent us from regarding them with fresh attention? Or does their character as sacred texts forbid an assessment in the general context of literature? Or do the gospels seem unpleasantly doctrinaire, tyrannical even? Perhaps the literary critics considered the gospels the exclusive domain of biblical scholars. Whatever the reasons for the neglect, the breakthrough toward a literary appreciation of the gospels, it is often said, came with Erich Auerbach's sensitive reading of Peter's

denial in Mark (1953: 24–49). In the wake of Auerbach, literary critics of
the stature of Robert Alter (1981), Frank Kermode (1979), and Herbert N.
Schneidau (1976; 1978; 1982; 1985) have recently turned to aspects of
biblical narrative to show how these perplexing and often disturbing texts
have informed Western literature and our sense of reality.

0.3   If until recently literary critics have left the gospels to the biblical
specialists, they were by and large left in the lurch. For although biblical
scholarship has for over two centuries subjected the gospels to exquisite
scrutiny, it has failed to grasp what matters most about them, their
narrative nature. Few theses proved as influential in setting hermeneutical standards as Papias' report concerning Mark's transcription of
Petrine teachings. It was widely understood to mean that the narrative
gospel resulted from preservation of unassimilated, uninterpreted information. Preservation from forgetfulness was assumed to be a prime
motive for the composition of the gospels, a concept prone to encourage
historical criticism more than narrative criticism. In the West, the rise of
idealistic philosophy and historical consciousness brought the interpretation of the gospels to a head. For the most part biblical interpreters
sought to distill from the gospels an ideational, preachable core or a
residue of verifiable fact. Hans Frei (1974) has documented the inability
of eighteenth and nineteenth century biblical hermeneutics to come to
terms with the gospels as realistic narratives. His report can and should
be extended into the twentieth century, for it was only in the last two
decades that biblical critics, mostly North Americans, began to appreciate the literary and rhetorical dimension of the gospels. At this point we
have only taken a very tentative step toward understanding the narrative
impulse in the early Christian tradition, the nature of the narrative
gospels, and our ways of interpreting them.

1.0   The impulse to narrate in the Christian tradition is frequently taken
as a matter of course. The gospels' life-to-death pattern, one of the most
common of all plot constructions, appears quintessentially like life itself
in moving toward death. What more natural beginning than birth, and
what more realistic ending than death! But no matter how natural or
realistic the narrative, artifice is unmistakably present, raising the issue
not of the represented world out there, but of how it is represented.
When it was recognized—rudimentarily by Papias, and also in Luke's
prologue—that the gospels originated out of tradition, pertinent questions as to the relationship between gospel and tradition tended to be
answered by the eye-witness theory. The death of the first generation of
witnesses was assumed to have prompted the writing of the gospel
narratives. Accordingly, a principal function of the gospels was to preserve the continuity of and with tradition. This theory lies at the root of
the popular (and to some extent still professional) paradigm of a single,
directional course of the tradition leading from the historical Jesus into

the written gospel. Form criticism, for all its methodological inadequacies, succeeded in alerting us to the significance of the tradition. If nothing else, the discipline sensitized us to the variability and complexity of the pre-gospel history of the tradition. Yet form criticism still operated under the presupposition of relatively uncomplicated gospel beginnings (Kelber, 1983: 1–43). Bultman assumed that the gospel narrated "nothing in principle new" that had not already been said by oral tradition (1970: 347 [1963: 321]). Birger Gerhardsson, who challenged form criticism, in effect bracketed the question of tradition by suggesting that the core of the narrative gospel had existed from the very outset (1961: 208–61; 262–323). In a far more subtly executed argument Paul Ricoeur has recently contended that the needs for narrativization, though not the narrative gospel itself, were inherent in the early Christian tradition from its inception (1984: 501–12). On all these views, the narrative impulse appears self-evident due to the facts or forces of tradition.

1.1   In seeking to account for the narrative gospel by appeal to tradition, one tends to disregard the diversity of traditions and the divergence of transmissional processes. Ricoeur is right in pointing to parable for the purpose of stressing the "requirement of narration internal to the proclamation itself" (1984: 511). Indeed, the parable joins proclamation to a story which, it has been suggested, became instrumental in the formation of the narrative gospel (Crossan, 1975: 10, 124; 1984: 15; Donahue, 1978; Kelber, 1983: 117–31). Yet parable is only one element in the tradition and commitment to narrative is only one trait of the tradition. The aphorisms of Jesus, for example, constitute non-narrative units, and the processes governing their transmission cannot be shown to generate the narrative gospel. In his recent book, *In Fragments* (1983), John D. Crossan has traced the conduct of synoptic aphorisms as they coalesce into compounds and clusters, become attached to stories, and develop into dialogues and series of dialogues[1]. As Crossan rightly saw, the aphoristic tendency toward clustering, dialogue, and discourse, while well recognizable in the orthodox tradition, became a generically fateful influence in what he calls the gnostic tradition (1983: 237, 268). What comes to mind are such documents as the *Gospel of Thomas*, the *Dialogue of the Savior*, the *Apocryphon of James*, and many others, and also Q, the sayings source, whose genre was, however, dispersed and displaced by Matthew and Luke. Is it permissible to discern in the aphoristic clustering a movement toward an alternate, a non-narrative gospel?

1.11   Few non-canonical documents have as great a potential for implementing a revision of our view of tradition as the *Gospel of Thomas*. This is all the more true if, as mounting evidence suggests, the bulk of Thomas is not only independent of the canonical gospels, but antecedent to them (Koester, 1971: 158–204; Davies, 1983: 3, *passim*). The document consists of single aphorisms, aphoristic and dialectical dialogues, and of parables, all spoken by the living Jesus. Strictly speaking it is not a consistently composed dialogue or discourse genre, and it "lacks" a unifying narrative setting. Whether the term *logoi* in the incipit (Oxy P 654) was the authentic designation of Thomas' genre (Robinson, 1971: 74–85), with *gospel* being secondarily appended as subscription so as to make *Thomas* competitive with the canonical gospels, or whether *gospel* was the authentic term for non-narrative *Thomas* (Vielhauer, 1975: 258, 622) has yet to be decided. The fact remains that *Thomas* was perceived quite early as a distinct genre, a sayings collection, and already in its Greek version understood to be a gospel, a sayings gospel (Robinson, 1971: 76). What we observe in this case is the principle of aphoristic clustering being carried to the point of generic consummation. When viewed from the standpoint of the *Gospel of Thomas*, therefore, the aphoristic behavior to cluster among its own kind appears in a fresh light. Now one may discern in it the potential for the production of a gospel *sui generis*. It is clear from this example that the needs for narrativization do not account for all the elements and proclivities of the tradition. The aphoristic proclamation may well have a momentum of its own toward a non-narrative genre, the sayings gospel.

1.12   The Nag Hammadi documents have brought into sharper focus the nature of the aphoristic processes vis-à-vis the narrative performance in emergent orthodoxy. When viewed from the canonical standpoint, it strikes one as remarkable how ill at ease these documents are with narrative syntax. In fact, none of these fifty-two texts comes even close to the genre of the orthodox gospel. Whereas the canonical gospels commence with birth or baptism, and end with resurrection, announced or fully narrated, or with ascension, the predominant generic proclivity at Nag Hammadi is toward the sayings discourse which stakes its authority on the teachings of the living or risen Jesus (Perkins, 1980). This quite extraordinary phenomenon deserves close scrutiny not only from those interested in linguistic aspects, but from those as well who explore the social world of early Christianity. What kind of communities (or perhaps worship situations) are we to imagine that showed such conspicuous partiality toward the aphoristic genre?

1.13   Based on these observations I have recently suggested that the time has come to draw a conclusion of considerable import for our understanding of the early Christian tradition[2]. Henceforth, we must reckon with two gospel genres in early Christianity, the sayings or cluster gospel, and the narrative gospel. The sayings or cluster gospel elevated the *logoi* proclamation to generic significance, promoting a Jesus who taught and redeemed through words of wisdom. The narrative gospel shaped a heterogeneous repertoire into biographical synthesis, favoring a Jesus who redeemed through the conduct of his life and death, followed by resurrection. Crossan, on the other hand, speaking at the same occasion[3], proposed the existence of three gospel genres: the cluster gospel, the dialogue gospel, and the narrative gospel. As aphoristic clustering furnished the condition for the sayings or cluster gospel, so did the aphoristic arrangement by way of comment/response or question/ answer format prepare for the dialogue gospel (*Dialogue of the Savior, Sophia of Jesus Christ*, etc.). Recognition of a duality, and perhaps even a plurality, of gospel genres compels us to contemplate the narrative gospel with renewed curiosity.

1.131 Perhaps agreement can be reached on the following four points. First, we may discern at least two, and possibly three, gospel genres, provided it is understood that both the cluster and the dialogue gospel arise out of the aphoristic processes, and that they are for this reason closely related, whereas the narrative gospel is generically unrelated to the aphoristic tradition. Second, the narrative gospel, the one genre accepted by orthodox Christianity for canonical inclusion, appears to be the formal heir not of the aphoristic processes, but of parable. Both in its narrative form and in its disorienting, metaphorical proclivity canonical Mark operates according to the hermeneutics of Jesus' parables. Third, it is tempting to speculate that each of the two basic speech forms attributable to the historical Jesus, the aphorism and the parable, were consummated in a gospel of its own: the aphorism in the sayings (and dialogue) gospel, and the parable in the narrative gospel. Fourth, while the sayings (and dialogue) gospel and the narrative gospel may each invoke continuity with Jesus, they grew out of different compositional needs and transmissional processes. Such are the differences in form, choice of materials, and christology that it is difficult, if not impossible, to assume direct, evolutionary connections between the aphoristic genre and the narrative genre. They will have developed separately, and they could well have existed in tension with each other.

1.2 If narrativity cannot be taken for granted in the early Christian tradition, neither can the strident tone in which it asserted itself in the canon. This point was reiterated by Elaine Pagels who after years of work on the Nag Hammadi texts continues to be astounded by the polemics of the canonical gospels: "The gospels which came to be accepted as orthodox generally interpret Jesus traditions in confrontational terms" (1981: 62). Her statement suggests that the gospels' polemics are occasioned by the manner in which these narratives relate to tradition. Preservation of traditions is not the sole purpose of the narrative gospels. I have recently sought to enlarge our understanding of the connections between Mark's deeply polemical narrative dynamics and antecedent traditions. I proposed that the canonical gospel form had arisen out of a conflict with the genre of the sayings gospel (1983: 90–139; 184–220). Mark's reserved attitude toward sayings (as compared to Matthew, Luke and John), the displacement of the vital oral authorities, the banishment of the Twelve to the outside, the extensive narrative explication of Jesus' earthly life, the narrative focus on his death, and a withholding of the living Lord are all features hostile to the genre built on sayings spoken by the living or risen Jesus. In the sayings gospel the living Jesus alone utters the words of life, whereas in Mark death puts an end to his speech. In terms of narrative form and focus, of christology, of principal features of dramatization, and of the rhetorical impact on hearers/readers the corrective function of the polemical narrative would seem to have plausibility. Methodologically, I wished to demonstrate that a gospel can (and should) be read both as a coherent narrative and in relation to tradition, whereby tradition is understood not only as a process of continuity, but in terms of discontinuity as well.

1.21   James Robinson, although pursuing a somewhat different intellectual path, has arrived at remarkably similar conclusions (1970: 99–129 [1982a: 11–39]; 1982b: 40–53; 1982c: 5–37). In his view, Mark's narrative genre must be understood in the context of "the bifurcating orthodox and gnostic positions" (1970: 114 [1982a: 27]). In what he calls the gnosticizing trajectory, the risen Christ, freed from bodily encumbrance and authorized by heavenly experiences, initiates "the time of a new hermeneutic as the time of the Spirit" (1982c: 26). Empowered by the Spirit, he speaks with authority, setting the norms of interpretation and initiating a period of higher revelation. In placing ultimacy upon the risen Christ, one tends to relegate to insignificance his earthly life "as just a lower and hence irrelevant prelude" (1970: 113 [1982a: 26]). Easter has thereby become the "time differential" (1982b: 48), i.e., the hermeneutical turning point separating a period or hermeneutic of concealment from the time or hermeneutic of revelation. Or, as gnosticizing texts tended to put it, prior to Easter Jesus spoke in riddling parables, but at Easter the risen Christ spoke "openly" (parrhēsia). Speaking "in parables" and speaking "openly" thereby became "the technical contrasting terms for designating the literal and spiritual levels of meaning . . . used to distinguish the sayings of Jesus before and after Easter" (1982c: 30). Parabolic speech, moreover, can itself be typical of Christ's post-Easter instruction imparted to a group of understanding disciples (1982b: 49). Insofar as the Christ of higher, esoteric revelation became the focal point for sayings and parables revealed to a select group of initiates, the gnosticizing trajectory was on its way toward the genre of the sayings and discourse gospel.

1.22   From the perspective of these gnosticizing proclivities Robinson finds sufficient clues in Mark to assume shifts from a post-Easter to a pre-Easter level of interpretation that are deeply connected with the genesis of the orthodox gospel. In Mark the period of higher revelation begins when Jesus announces his first passion-resurrection prediction by speaking "openly" (Mk 8:32: *parrhēsia*). In this case the gnosticizing "'Easter' shift" (1970: 111 [1982a: 29]) has been retrojected into the pre-Easter period. Consequently, the higher revelation is refocused from the parables and sayings spoken by the living Jesus to the earthly Jesus and the proclamation of his death and also resurrection. It is this orthodox emphasis on death followed by resurrection that accounts for Mark's focused narrative engagement in the passion. One might add that it also clarifies the absence and silence of the risen Christ. If death is the point of higher revelation then the earthly Jesus has already said and accomplished all that matters. Another feature involved in shifting perspectives is the transfiguration long suspected of being a transposed resurrection story (Bultmann, 1970: 278 [1963: 259]). Robinson, confirming the thesis, draws attention to the analogous gnosticizing type of apparition story (1970: 116–18 [1982a: 29–31]). Many gnostic gospels are cast in the form of a luminous epiphany of the risen Lord on a mountain. Based on this analogy, the transfiguration has all the appearances of an apparition story relocated in close proximity to the new hermeneutical turning point, the first passion-resurrection prediction. Jesus' esoteric instruction in parables (Mk 4:1–34) likewise shows traces of a pre-Markan functioning (1982b: 43–47). It resembles precisely the kind of higher revelation that in the gnosticizing genre is reserved for the post-Easter disciples. In Mark, however, the esoteric instruction is purposefully undermined "in that the disciples, in spite of the interpretation, remain as much in the dark as do the outsiders" (1970: 112 [1982a: 25]). These and other observations suggest to Robinson that in Mark "Easter material is embedded back into the public ministry" (1982b: 52) with the intent to refocus or correct the gnosticizing trajectory by placing the highest revelatory premium on the earthly Jesus and his death. According to Robinson's well-known formula, " . . . gnosticism's Gospel *Gattung* begins just as regularly after the resurrection as the orthodox *Gattung* ends there" (1970: 114 [1982a: 27]). When thus examined in the light of bifurcating traditions the narrative gospel presents itself as an attempt on the part of emergent orthodoxy to block the gnosticizing sayings genre and to assert itself "as a replacement for the all too ambivalent Q" (1982c: 37).

1.23   Yet another approach that arrived at a similar assessment of Mark's gospel was undertaken by Eugene Boring (1982). He proceeded from early Christian prophecy and its modes of discourse. A distinctive feature of early Christian prophets, according to Boring, was their role as inspired spokesmen of the risen Lord. Conscious of being commissioned by the Lord, they spoke his sayings in his name and on his authority. The hermeneutical rationale for prophetic speech was not, therefore, to preserve the teachings of the Jesus of the past, but to keep his voice and authority alive in the community. This study of the prophetic function of (many of) the synoptic sayings brings Boring finally to posit his thesis concerning the genesis of the narrative gospel. Mark carries only a little more than half as many sayings as either Matthew or Luke. Apart from the eschatological discourse, Boring can identify only five of Mark's sayings as prophetic speech (1982: 183–203). In addition, Boring sees Mark withholding all sayings from the risen Lord. The latter "is not only absent, he is silent" (1977: 377 [1982: 203]). When viewed against the prophetic mode of representing Jesus' sayings as an address of the living Lord, the purpose and achievement of the narrative gospel appears in a new light. Both the gospel's paucity of sayings and its scarcity of specifically prophetic sayings, and also its ending at 16:8, which confines traditions to a strictly pre-Easter framework, find an explanation in Mark's intention to compose an alternate form to the prophetically functioning sayings tradition. Mark's achievement was to curb the prophetic use of sayings as post-Easter revelation of the living or risen Jesus by creating the pre-Easter form which endorses the earthly Jesus.

1.24   The fact that Robinson, Boring and my own recent work regard the narrative gospel as a corrective to the type of sayings genre weighs all the more heavily in that we proceeded largely independently and with the aid of different methods. Robinson took his cue from William Wrede (1901 [1981]), critically advancing his epochal work, *Das Messiasgeheimnis in den Evangelien*, with fresh insights derived from the Nag Hammadi documents. Boring undertook a study of early Christian prophecy from its beginnings up to the formation of the narrative gospels. My own, more theoretically conceived work developed the early Christian hermeneutics of orality versus textuality. Whether one understands the narrative gospel as a corrective to the gnosticizing trajectory, or as an attempt to control prophetic speech and revelations, or as a rigorous application of textuality versus an oral ontology of language, all three of us view the narrative gospel as a reaction to, or reinterpretation of an antecedent stage in the tradition.

1.3   If we now include in our reflections the vital aspect of speech in the tradition, a model of three orders of operation suggests itself: orality, the sayings genre, and the narrative gospel. This model is not intended to impute a sense of evolutionary ascendancy to tradition, as if it were propelled by inexorable regularity to move from speech to the sayings gospel only to peak in narrativity. Orality, sayings gospel, and narrative gospel are meant to be viewed as characteristic components in the tradition, not as sequential stages in an orderly process. After all, the issue of narrativity was already entrusted to tradition with parabolic speech; the sayings gospel flourished before, concurrently with, and after the canonical gospels; and speech remained a fertile ground all along. Indeed, the most difficult part of the tradition to understand may be the interactions that existed not only between texts and texts, but the recycling of texts into speech, the transformation of speech into writing, and an oral remembering and dismembering of texts, all processes little or not at all understood in biblical scholarship. As a possible step toward clarifying the role of gospel narrativity in the tradition, however, the model of the three orders may prove helpful.

1.31 The tradition commenced with aphorisms and parables, the two units attributable to the historical Jesus. It would seem inescapably obvious that they are primary phenomena of speech. As such they inhabit a world quite different from words that are fixed on papyrus to be seen. In the oral world, aphorisms and parables operate largely on acoustical principles. They constitute speech acts, consisting of pitches and pauses, stresses and silence. "In oral speech, the sound is the sign of the meaning" (Havelock, 1978: 231). Put differently, meaning is a kind of rhythmic envelope. As long as aphorism and parable function orally, one may speak of a *first order of operation*. Although it is true that written words "are on the whole far more likely to be misunderstood than spoken words are" (Ong, 1967: 115), hermeneutical complications were an inalienable part of oral tradition. Parables in particular placed into tradition from its inception the need for interpretation. Their metaphorical and withholding proclivities encouraged notions of secrecy, of insider versus outsider, and of revealing versus concealing. "Their kinship with the enigma cannot be too strongly emphasized" (Ricoeur, 1975: 133). "He who has ears to hear, let him hear." But how does one hear parabolic story, and what did the parabolist intend to convey? Questions of this kind launch the process of interpretation. But in the first order of operation interpretation is not linked to fixed parable texts in the manner of Mark who attached interpretive discourse to the parable of the Sower. The oral transaction of aphorisms and parables consists in multiple recitals, tailored to specific circumstances, without the auditors ever hearing them as departures from binding texts. In the absence of aphoristic and parabolic texts one does not trade in originals and variants thereof. One knows no way of testing speech against fixed models. But the condition of interpretation exists from the outset, forcing hearers to wonder and ponder, and the parabolist to adapt and restate.

1.32 With clustering a *second order of operation* gets under way. Aphorisms and parables were collected and placed one next to the other in cluster arrangements or in dialogues set in slim narrative frames. Pheme Perkins, virtually the only New Testament scholar to use the categories developed by Walter Ong, has suggested that the genre of the revelation dialogue still operates within the conventions of oral tradition. Indeed, many of the Gnostic writings that have come to light at Nag Hammadi attracted predominantly speech material much of which reflects "the liturgy, teaching, preaching and polemic of their respective communities" (1980: 201). In the case of the sayings and dialogue genres, Jesus' oral proclamation, his very spoken words, had fashioned for themselves gospels in their own right. Their primary interest was neither philosophical, nor cosmological, but soteriological. To this end they sought to retain the living voice of Jesus and to extend it into the communal present. Yet all of this was accomplished through writing, and writing is deconstructive to the vital concerns of orality. While aphorisms and parables generally retained their oral form, a specific stage of the tradition was frozen, inviting comparison and disclosing thereby the interpretive nature of its materials. Wisdom showed itself to be the focal point of the *Gospel of Thomas*, and Son of Man apocalypticism of Q. The principle of clustering itself is not in the best interest of orality. As far as is known, oral conventions do not favor speaking in clusters of like materials. The compilation of sayings and parables, a textually contrived arrangement, invites reflection and analysis, further heightening the sense of interpretation. In this second order of operation interpretation becomes a self-conscious activity. This is evident from the first saying of the *Gospel of Thomas* which summons hearers to the task of interpretation: "Whoever finds the explanation of these words will not taste death." The one hundred and fourteen sayings of Thomas require interpretation (*hermeneia*), and finding interpretation is perceived to be a matter of life and death. Despite the textual aspects of the sayings and dialogue genres, one must be mindful of the oral context of their functioning. The communities in which they originated did not look upon texts as the normative source of revelation and interpretation. While these gospels contained true tradition and continued the voice of Jesus, "truth is not [understood to be] definitively embodied in an inspired text. Gnostic interpretation is still the hermeneutic of an oral tradition" (Perkins, 1980: 202). In different words, what mattered most was the experience of the Christ, of the Kingdom, or of Wisdom.

1.33 While the second order was *(inter alia)* committed to the two authentic speech acts, the narrative gospel in turn deprived aphorisms and parables of their oral status by subordinating them, together with a good deal of additional materials, to the literary ordering of narrative. When reflecting, therefore, on the synoptic tradition from the perspective of its vital oral inception, something in the nature of a mutation suggests itself in the shifting from the second to the third order. Orality, the voice of the living Jesus, the ground and life of the tradition, and the very gospels of Jesus' proclamation were overruled by the more complex ordering of narrative textuality. It is, on this view, not entirely surprising that the *third order of operation*, the narrative configuration, asserted itself canonically in tension with the second order. Interpretation further intensified on this level. Insofar as Mark enacted an alternative to the sayings gospel, his narrative accomplished the interpretation of an interpretation. Ironically, Mark redescribed the second order genre via the dynamics of parabolic reversal (Kelber, 1983: 117–29). The narrative gospel reversed the inside view so as to subvert conventional expectations, and placed an additional burden on its hearers/readers by forestalling closure. It was precisely this parabolic posture of the Markan narrative that solicited further interpretation. Here we can see how a narrative that had already come into existence by virtue of reinterpretation was itself destined to engender more interpretation. When viewed from the perspective of tradition history, therefore, Matthew and Luke are interpretations of the interpretation (= Mark) of an interpretation (= sayings gospel). Both Matthew and Luke domesticated the Markan narrative, blunting its parabolic edges and furnishing closure. No longer faced with Mark's task of correcting the sayings genre, they could open their gospels more readily to aphorisms and parables. The latter, however, had to comply with the rules of their respective narrative houses. In the end, orthodoxy would disallow the sayings gospel as a genre in its own right, and would admit the second and first order of operation into the canon only through mediation of the third order. Narrative, the most thoroughly textualized piece, emerged as the victor in the canonical ratification of the synoptic tradition.

1.4   The time has come to include in our reflections a controversial item which, if proven authentic, further complicates our thinking about the tradition and the role of narrative within it. Our reference is to the *Secret Gospel of Mark*. Space compels us to confine the review of this intricate case to its barest essentials. The discovery of *Secret Mark* dates back to 1958 when Morton Smith came across an incomplete copy of a letter of Clement of Alexandria at the Greek orthodox monastery of Mar Saba in the Judean desert (1973a; 1973b; 1982:449–61). In this letter, written to an otherwise unknown Theodore, Clement cites a portion of *Secret Mark*. It is the story of a rich, young man whom Jesus raises from the dead. Having been brought back to life, he loves Jesus and beseeches him that he might be with him. "After six days" the youth, "wearing a linen cloth over his naked body," spends a night with Jesus to be initiated into "the mystery of the Kingdom of God." Clement himself proposed that *Secret Mark* was a revision of canonical Mark, a view to some extent shared by Smith (1973a: 142; 1973b: 145, 163, 194)[4]. More recently, however, first Helmut Koester (1983: 35–57) and then Crossan (1985: 91–121) have advocted a reversal of the compositional sequence: canonical Mark has revised *Secret Mark*. Canonical Mark's revision is assumed to have been motivated by the Carpocratians who gave the resurrection-baptismal story in *Secret Mark* a homosexual slant in the fashion of gnostic libertinism. Faced with an exceedingly delicate situation, Mark proceeded to eliminate the explosive story by dismemberment and redistribution. In other words, canonical Mark is assumed to have scattered its textual debris across his own text. The naked young man now appears at the arrest (Mk 14:51–52), the motif of love is transferred to the story of the

Rich Man and rephrased in the sense that Jesus loved him and not the reverse (Mk 10:17–22; cf. 10:21), the six days are connected with the transfiguration (Mk 9:2), the mystery of the Kingdom is relocated after public parable (4:11), and so forth. Having thus decomposed the controversial text, canonical Mark appears to have successfully met the Carpocratian scandal, for their erotic version would henceforth give the impression of having been secondarily produced out of bits and pieces from canonical Mark.

1.41   Bearing in mind that *Secret Mark* poses uncommonly labyrinthian problems that await a good deal more philological, text critical, and historical work, we may at this stage draw four preliminary conclusions. First, there may well have been more narrative in the tradition prior to canonical Mark. What comes to mind is the astute, though very scribally based, observation made by the monk Adso of Melk in Umberto Eco's *The Name of the Rose* (1983: 286) and cited as second epigraph to this piece. Texts are never simply created out of lived experience, least of all perhaps biblical texts which are multifariously enmeshed in tradition. It appears likely that there existed something of a Markan school tradition not unlike the one we have long recognized with respect to the Johannine materials. If *Secret Mark* indeed has priority over canonical Mark, we can only specualte as to the narrative impulse of the former. Our knowledge of the history of the synoptic tradition should caution us against assuming that in *Secret Mark* we have arrived at "pure" narrative equivalent to the bedrock of history. As Clement himself seems to indicate, the setting of *Secret Mark* was the Alexandrian baptismal ritual. Second, although we have known of the gospels' involvement in tradition, canonical Mark may be more deeply and actively engaged than we ever thought possible. It can never be sufficiently stressed that fidelity to the *history* of its subject matter cannot account for the canonical narrative. I suspect we will increasingly find dependencies and displacement features in canonical Mark that testify to his wrestling with traditions. Crossan has reason to assert that canonical Mark was not only decomposing the resurrection-baptismal story of *Secret Mark*, but that he was also redacting *Egerton Papyrus 2* (1985: 65–87) and revising the passion narrative of the *Gospel of Peter* (1985: 125–35). In all this Crossan sees intertextuality triumphing in the tradition. Yet the principle of intertextuality, far from being simply a matter of hard evidence, is also a presupposition of our method. Trained to interpret texts, impressed by the ubiquity of texts, and working single-mindedly with texts, we are bound to discover intertextuality. But how is one to imagine—technically, psychologically, religiously—Mark's skillful juggling of a number of texts, using them, revising them, deconstructing them, while all along composing an impressively coherent narrative? Are we not asking canonical Mark to juggle too many balls at once? At any rate, the larger the number of traditions we find canonical Mark coping with, the less persuasive or imaginable the principle of intertextuality becomes. Third, if canonical Mark does interact with multiple traditions, oral apperception would seem to be the most plausible procedure. How could he have laboriously picked first from one text, then from another, revised one scrap of papyrus, and scattered another? He is more likely to have operated from a memory that was in possession of a plurality of traditions. What to us textually bound scholars appears to be tight intertextuality, may in hermeneutical actuality have been free composition, "especially in antiquity, when most writers, even in citing explicitly, cited from memory" (Smith, 1973b: 143). Of all the traditions canonical Mark may have displaced, the genre of a sayings gospel still is my favorite candidate. Its deconstruction best explains the genre of the canonical narrative. Fourth, is Clement's view of the priority of canonical Mark over *Secret Mark* beyond all redemption? What if the naked young man at the arrest, owing to his enigmatic presence in the narrative, gave rise to the resurrection-baptismal story in *Secret Mark* on the one hand and to the Lazarus story in John on the other? If, in different words, Mk 14:51–52 was experienced as a narrative secret, an "indeterminacy gap," one proven way of coping with it is more narrative[5].

2.0   A reading of gospel narrativity from the angle of tradition history is currently not much in favor with many biblical critics who have embarked upon a literary examination of narrative. The study of the interior narrative world is now widely held to be incompatible with reflection on its possible involvement in tradition. What cannot under any circumstances be questioned is the significance of our growing sensitivity to the narrative quality of the gospels. The issue here is the tendency among literary critics of the Bible to assign priority in rank (Petersen, 1978; Alter, 1981) or in operation (Polzin, 1980; Culpepper, 1983) to the literary vis-á-vis the historical study of narrative. To read narrative texts both as "mirrors" reflecting self-contained worlds and as "windows" opening upon the pre-narrative history seems to be almost a violation of proper hermeneutical conduct. It is not entirely clear, however, whether biblical hermeneutics is categorically divisible into the literary versus the historical mode of interpretation, one having precedence over the other. Murray Krieger, from whom we borrowed the metaphors of "mirror" and "window," sought to maintain their simultaneous functioning so that meaning arises "not just *through* the work and not just *in* the work but at once *through* and *in* the work as body" (1964: 28)[6]. Following Krieger's critical theory, perhaps we can arrive at a more judicious, less apodictic assessment of literary criticism, if we locate the latter in the broader context of cultural, linguistic developments. If, for example, one traces the cultural history in terms of orality, scribality, and typography, then literary criticism in the exclusivist, "mirror" sense described above is

most closely allied with typography, the phase dominated by printing.
This deserves some explication.

2.1 The existence of speech appears odd when viewed from a literary
perspective, because it "lacks" a visual, objectifiable presence. Oral
words cannot be locked into space. They are uncontainable in formal,
visual models. Bound to the authority of the speaker and inseparable
from auditors, they are inevitably enmeshed in the human lifeworld. To
regard spoken words as knowable in terms strictly of themselves and as
operable apart from historical contextuality is a notion that has no conceivable reality in oral culture. Oral utterance cannot exist in transauthorial objectivity (Tyler, 1978, *passim;* Ong, 1982: 5–77; Kelber, 1983:
44–89). Speech, we observed (cf. 1.31), is rhythmically structured sound
and it acquires meaning as a contextual phenomenon. We must add here
a caveat against an understanding of orality strictly in terms of sound,
rhythm, acoustics and human contextuality. Both ancient and medieval
oral culture exhibited a visual element as well, not of course in the sense
of external visualization of speech through writing, but as an inner
visualization (Yates, 1966). Mnemotechnics did not facilitate instant recall
simply based on sound tracks drilled into the mind. They also involved
the formation of memory images, i.e., heroic figures, dramatic scenes,
striking places, etc. The ideal was to express everything one wanted
hearers to retain in a way that encouraged imaging. A flourishing of
imagination and visions, a rich inner visualized world, was an essential
part of ancient oral operations.

2.2 With scribality the shift from sound to sight, i.e., external visualization, gets under way. Words written down enjoy a stable existence denied
to spoken words. Demands on the *vis vivendi*, the most discriminating of
the senses, intensify in scribal culture. "The eye lends distance to things, it
makes them into objects" (Snell, 1960: 33). Detachment, objectivity,
abstraction, and introspection, all virtuous contributions to the civilizing
process, benefit from the shift to scribality. The art of memory, however,
the life of visions and imagination (= the making of inner images)
declines[7]. And yet, the notion that texts, laboriously manufactured
(= handmade), relate interiorly back unto themselves, and only to themselves, is foreign to scribal hermeneutics. Contemporary scholars living
in a typographically dominant civilization have rarely been trained to
appreciate the ancient and medieval manuscript culture except through a
consciousness shaped by the invention of printing. In her monumental
work, *The Printing Press as an Agent of Change* (1979), Elizabeth Eisenstein made the point that it is easier for us print-oriented people to
understand orality than to grasp medieval, let alone ancient, scribality:

> The gulf that separates our experience from that of literate élites
> who relied exclusively on hand-copied texts is much more difficult

to fathom. There is nothing analogous in our experience or in that
of any living creature within the Western world at present. The
conditions of scribal culture thus have to be artificially reconstructed by recourse to history books and reference guides. Yet
for the most part, these works are more likely to conceal than to
reveal the object of such a search. Scibal themes are carried
forward, postprint trends are traced backward in a manner that
makes it difficult to envisage the existence of a distinctive literary
culture based on hand-copying (1979, I: 9).

Manuscripts in scribal culture were not under the spell of the objectifying standards set by printing or high technology (Eisenstein, 1979, I,
II; Stock, 1983). Rarely, if ever, were ancient texts thought to be fully
closed, and rarely, if ever, was a narrative text viewed as a hall of mirrors,
reflecting nothing but internal relations. Both manufacture and use of
manuscripts readily interacted with orality, be it through dictation or
recitation. That most ancient manuscripts were meant to reach out
toward readers, or more likely hearers, so as to influence their views and
play on their emotions, is something reception theorists have discovered
only recently (Iser, 1974; 1978; Link, 1976; Fish, 1980; Jauss, 1982). Yet
what today we call reader-response criticism was part of scribal hermeneutics which by and large was still committed to the art of persuasion
and unfriendly toward fully closed systems. This relative hermeneutical
openness applies with special force to biblical manuscripts (Ong, 1977:
230–71; Bruns, 1982: 17–59). Whether prose or poetry, epistle or narrative, wisdom or apocalypse, biblical texts aim at being heard, read, and
actualized. More often than not they are the products of rewriting
themselves, and in turn they can be subject to revisions (cf. 1.33).
"Scripture is something that is always turning into new versions of itself"
(Bruns, 1982: 26). And revising in biblical hermeneutics is not bound by
modern standards of literalness, but inspired by a passion for vivification
through inspiration.
2.3   With printing technical control over words reached a state of perfec-
tion unimaginable in chirographic culture. More than ever words took on
the appearance of autosemantic objectivity. "Print encouraged the mind
to sense that its possessions were held in some sort of inert mental space"
(Ong, 1982:132). Centuries of interiorization of typographical consciousness gave birth to the Saussurian principle of integrity of language
whereby meaning is figured as relations within language and not as
reference to something outside it. Both the Russian formalism and the so-
called New Criticism, while originating independently, epitomized typography in advocating the transauthorial autonomy of texts. In the light
of these critical disciplines narrative was understood as a system of
interrelations rather than as a product of causes. Structuralism pene-

trated the interior world of texts ever more deeply. With respect to
narrative, the hidden structure was given priority at the expense of the
plotted storyline. Genetic considerations were held to be irrelevant at
worst and secondary at best as far as a proper understanding of narrative
was concerned. Here we have come full circle back to our earlier observation about the hermetic, "mirror" type of literary criticism being a
favorite child of typography (cf. 2.0). When placed in the broader context
of cultural, linguistic processes, literary criticism of the formalist type
appears to be flourishing at a stage in intellectual history when the
technologizing, objectifying impact of printing has culminated in the
apotheosis of the text as a closed system. Many biblical critics who have
lately adopted literary criticism, adopted it in this formalist mode. We
turned to it enthusiastically, though somewhat unreflectively, out of
disillusionment with centuries of grossly referential hermeneutics (Frei,
1974). In this situation, biblical narrative and even parable (Via, 1967)
were appreciated as self-referential entities, standing entirely on their
own as aesthetic objects[8].

2.4   What bears repeating is the significance of the literary assessment
of the gospels. The analysis of the narrative nature of the gospels is not
only justifiable, it is imperative. In view of the long dominance of the
historical paradigm in gospel studies, literary criticism truly marks a
Copernican revolution. Our task now is to move beyond formalism in
literary theory and practice, although not in the sense of retreating to the
older historical, philological model of interpretation. "A crucial test of the
viability of contemporary criticism is whether it can formulate a program
of literary history that uses the strengths of formalism and yet avoids its
current impasse" (Hoy, 1978: 9). To this end literary critics of the gospels
should become more circumspect about the degree to which not only
narrative, the object of their study, but all our ways of approaching
narrative and literature are inescapably bound up with language and its
technological developments. Once we learn to see distinctions between a
chirographically and a typographically informed hermeneutic, and grasp
a sense of the hermeneutics of revisionism and vivification typical of
ancient, biblical manuscripts, might we not grow more tolerant methodologically, acknowledging the gospels both as integral narratives and as
narrative participants in tradition, as documents both of synchronic integrity and diachronic depth? Or, to put it more provocatively, are not the
gospels both "windows" and "mirrors" giving us worlds that interact with
other worlds? In any case, fear of the "referential fallacy" should not
cause us to disclaim the manifold ties the gospels have with tradition, for
no text is composed in complete referential neutrality, not in antiquity,
least of all in the biblical tradition.

2.41   To say that the gospels work out of and respond to tradition is to
suggest the possibility of undertaking the study of narrativity and tradi-

tion historical analysis as mutually enriching and corrective enterprises. This is precisely what David C. Hoy has suggested in the fourth epigraph to this piece. On the one hand comprehension of a gospel's linguistic and narrative world could well serve to revise our view of its relation to tradition. If, for example, a stylistically and literarily sensitive examination of the fourth gospel were to show that the so-called aporias, i.e., ideological, stylistic, and contextual discrepancies, are integral to John's narrative rhetoric, a vital argument for the existence of the *Gospel of Signs* (Fortna, 1970) would be called into question. Whatever the eventual outcome of the assumed *Gospel of Signs*, repetition of catch-words and phrases, a notable feature of Fortna's reconstruction, is dubious evidence for editorial activity. For redundancy, which in various degrees is common to all canonical gospels, is first and foremost an index of the rhetorical style of ancient narrative prose. What to our modern perception of the flow of realistic narrative appears to be "repetition," was to the ancients a conventional, hearer-friendly mode of composition. Hence, an analysis of the interior gospel world may aid us in shaping, or even challenging, a view of tradition.

2.42   On the other hand, familiarity with a feature of tradition may illuminate gospel narrativity. Discipleship in Mark, for example, is intelligible up to a point as a particular narrative enactment. Dan Via chose to interpret it as a pattern of contrast whereby the disciples act out the role of alazoon-opponents vis-à-vis the agonist-hero. It is a role primarily conditioned by the dramatic structure of comedy, and only secondarily, if at all, by pressures outside of narrative (1975: 45, 117). Joanna Dewey has carried the hermetic hermeneutics of narrative to its radical conclusion in suggesting that the key to discipleship in Mark was to be found nowhere but "in the needs of the narrative itself" (1984: 13). Since story thrives on conflict, and the disciples do their very best to produce conflict, their role is intelligible as "the result of telling the gospel in the form of a story" (1984: 13). If, however, we rest content with the assumption that the disciples' conflict is narrated merely for the purpose of fulfilling narrative requirements, we deprive, or rather protect, ourselves from raising deeper questions. To be sure, inasmuch as discipleship can be shown to fulfill a particular narrative emplotment, such as role reversal from insiders to outsiders, its function in the gospel is understood. But the very logic of that emplotment, far from settling all our questions, prompts further inquiries. Whence this boldness to narrate the disciples' dysfunctional role? Why cast the very ones to the outside who are known to the narrator as the appointed insiders? Although we may know the mechanics of the discipleship plot, we still lack an answer concerning its motive. These are questions intrinsic to the narrative, yet not susceptible of explanation in terms of the narrative itself. If answers are not forthcoming from the interiority of the narrative, are we not entitled to turn to the larger frame of reference, and to take note of narrative and tradition as intersecting worlds?

2.421   There is one component in the discipleship narration that Mark appears to have retrieved from tradition: the disciples' role as privileged insiders. The spotlight inevitably falls on Mk 4:1–34, the first of two major sayings collections in the gospel. The pre-Markan formation of the core of this collection is almost universally acknowledged, though details of the reconstruction remain controversial. Here we encounter Jesus as speaker of parables and aphorisms, and the Twelve as privileged insiders. If one replaces the earthly Jesus with the living Lord, we have in fact arrived at a miniature model of the sayings gospel, or, in Robinson's words, at the "immediate precursor of the Gospel of Thomas," where "much of this material recurs" (1982b: 47). Once we become sensitive to Mark's involvement in tradition, or rather, to the traces tradition has left in Mark, it will no longer do to attribute the discipleship plot simply to the pleasure of telling a good story. For now we can read Mark's reversal of the disciples' fate as a subversion of the scenario of a sayings gospel. Given Mark's singular narrative focus on Jesus' earthly life culminating in death, the withholding of the risen Lord, and a reservation toward sayings, the reversal of the role of the disciples must not entirely surprise us, for all these features converge in revising the posture of a sayings gospel. In different words, Mark's narrative emplotment of discipleship is part and parcel of a revisionist text. We have arrived at an understanding of the mechanism of and the motivation for the discipleship plot in Mark. This goes to show that tradition history may indeed play a part in illuminating our understanding of gospel narrativity.

3.0   As literary criticism of the gospels commences in earnest, we do well not to lose sight of the interdependence that exists between the canonical narratives and the wider orbit of tradition. Exclusive attention to internal, synchronic relations is less than faithful to scribal hermeneutics. It may also, unwittingly perhaps, introduce a false sense of foundationalism. When viewed from the diachronic perspective, the gospels reveal their interpretive status. They came into being under the pressures of interpretation. Whatever authority they exude, and however foundational an impression they may create, each gospel is bound up with a process of interpretive traditioning. Given this state of affairs, anything resembling a foundational level is likely to elude us, whether it be that of history, or of uninterpreted narrative. The first time we encounter narrative in the full light of canonicity, we encounter it not as the ground of tradition, but as a pattern of elementary tensions. It represents a revisionist text, intent in displacing the genre of the sayings gospel, and perhaps of other gospels. When Robinson referred to the transfiguration story as belonging to a tradition "suppressed in orthodox

Christianity, and surviving in the New Testament canon only indirectly, at mislocated positions" (1970: 117–18 [1982a: 30]), he was employing, quite appropriately, the language of revisionist hermeneutics: suppression, indirect survival, and mislocation. Freud, who taught us much about the mechanisms of displacement and revisionism, knew that many precursors will not simply vanish into the night of anonymity; their traces remain hidden in the revisionist text (Freud, 1900; 1939; Handelman, 1982). This is his message in the third epigraph to this piece. In the *Gospel of Thomas* a strong precursor has literally returned, challenging conventional views of the traditioning process and of the rise of the narrative gospel. Strong precursors have a way of coming back, disclosing the present as displacement of the past.

3.1 Narrative as interpretation is a notion that readily crosses boundaries we have come to take for granted. If the canonical narrative was itself born in the act of interpretation, then readers faced with interpreting this narrative persist in an activity that is observable not only in Mark, but as far back as tradition will take us. Whether in our time we interpret by reading or preaching, through books or commentary, by augmentation or radical revision of anteriority, we are in the process of perpetuating interpretation. Both narrator-as-interpreter and interpreters of narrative jointly partake in the embracing activity of hermeneutical translations. This hermeneutical condition, perceptively formulated by Kermode in the last epigraph, has been elevated by Gadamer to the level of an epistemological principle. As such it forms the leading epigraph to our piece. It would not seem feasible, from this perspective, to draw a firm line between the literary study of the gospels and the historical analysis of their tradition history. For what distinguishes the canonical gospels from what preceded them is not primarily a matter of literature versus history, but rather one of interpretation turning canonical. Canonicity, far from terminating the interpretive impulse, assured survival of the narrative gospel in prestigious position, thus rendering it normative for the continuing history of interpretation. Nor can a categorical distinction be drawn between the gospels as mirrors vis-à-vis windows. Precisely because they participate in the ongoing discourse of tradition, narrative gospels contain traces of absent others, which, while integrated into their respective gospel worlds, may serve as windows for those who know the scope of the tradition. When viewed from these perspectives, therefore, opposites such as narrative versus interpretation, literary versus historical readings, and mirror versus window views of language dissolve into the single, overriding reality of interpretation. And interpretation is more than a matter of method, and more than a manifestation of madness. It is rather our essential mode of survival.

NOTES

[1] For an extensive discussion of Crossan's *In Fragments*, see my review essay, "From Aphorism to Sayings Gospel, and from Parable to Narrative Gospel," in *FFF* (= *Facets and Foundations Forum*) 1 (1985): 1–8.

[2] Werner H. Kelber, "The Gospels as Stories," presentation at SBL/AAR/ASOR Annual Meeting, Chicago, IL, December 1984, in session on *Biblical Criticism and Literary Criticism*, presiding William A. Beardslee.

[3] John D. Crossan, "Language and Creativity: Jesus as Aphorist and Parabler," presentation at SBL/AAR/ASOR Annual Meeting, Chicago, IL, December 1984, in session on *Biblical Criticism and Literary Criticism*, presiding William A. Beardslee.

[4] According to Morton Smith's own judgment, his *Clement of Alexandria and the Secret Gospel of Mark* is "a dreadfully complex book" (1982: 456). If I understand his central thesis correctly, *Secret Mark* is an imitation of canonical Mark with additional elements, such as the resurrection-baptismal story, that were taken from a pre-canonical Markan gospel.

[5] The term "indeterminacy gap" is derived from Kermode (1983: 128) who credits Roman Ingarten with its formulation. It directs attention to the lack of narrative connexity. In the history of interpretation, "indeterminacy gaps" cry out for fillings with narrative sequence, and "a passion for sequence may result in the suppression of the secret" (1983: 138).

[6] Krieger developed his thesis of the functional simultaneity of mirror and window in working with poetry. I see no reason why it should not be equally applicable to biblical narrative.

[7] Frances A. Yates (1966, *passim*) offers a brilliant explanation of the decline of the interiorly imaged world in the 16th century and the corresponding iconoclasm, i.e., the destruction of external images. With the Reformation memory was omitted from the discipline of rhetoric. The omission was, of course, closely linked with the invention of printing and an increased availability of pamphlets and books. What happened in Calvinism, and to some extent in Lutheranism, was a projection of the interior erasure toward the outside resulting in the demolition of pictures that were often the artistic outcome of inner imaging: ". . . there can be no doubt that an art of memory based on imageless dialectical order as the true natural order of the mind goes well with Calvinist theology" (1966: 237).

[8] The contemporary electronics revolution produces novel alliances of sound and vision, a reassembling of the economy of the senses, and a breakdown of closed model thinking. Perhaps these cultural developments are not entirely unconnected with the rediscovery of the communicative, hearer and reader oriented function of texts (cf. 2.2).

WORKS CONSULTED

Alter, Robert
    1981   *The Art of Biblical Narrative*. New York: Basic Books.
Auerbach, Erich
    1953   *Mimesis. The Representation of Reality in Western Literature*.
                Princeton, N.J.: Princeton University Press.
Barthes, Roland
    1977   *Image—Music—Text*. New York: Hill & Wang.
Boring, M. Eugene
    1977   "The Paucity of Sayings in Mark: A Hypothesis." Pp. 371–77 in
                SBL Seminary Papers. Missoula, MT: Scholars Press.
    1982   *Sayings of the Risen Jesus. Christian Prophecy in the Synoptic*

Tradition. SNTS MS 46. Cambridge: Cambridge University Press.

Bruns, Gerald L.
1982   *Inventions. Writing, Textuality, and Understanding in Literary History.* New Haven and London: Yale University Press.

Bultmann, Rudolf
1970   *Die Geschichte der synoptischen Tradition. FRLANT* 29, *NF* 12. 8th ed. Göttingen: Vandenhoeck & Ruprecht [Eng. trans., *The History of the Synoptic Tradition.* New York: Harper & Row, 1963].

Crossan, John Dominic
1975   *The Dark Interval. Towards a Theology of Story.* Niles, IL: Argus Communications.
1983   *In Fragments. The Aphorisms of Jesus.* San Francisco: Harper & Row.
1984   "Language and Creativity. Jesus as Aphorist and Parabler." Presentation at SBL/AAR/ASOR Annual Meeting in Chicago, IL.
1985   *Four Other Gospels. Shadows on the Contours of Canon.* Minneapolis, MN: Winston Press.

Culpepper, R. Alan
1983   *Anatomy of the Fourth Gospel. A Study in Literary Design.* Philadelphia: Fortress Press.

Davies, Stevan L.
1983   *The Gospel of Thomas and Christian Wisdom.* New York: Seabury Press.

Dewey, Joanna
1984   "Literary Criticism and the Gospels: Meaning in Narrative." Unpublished paper.

Eco, Umberto
1983   *The Name of the Rose.* San Diego, CA: Harcourt Brace Jovanovich.

Eisenstein, Elizabeth L.
1979   *The Printing Press as an Agent of Change. Communications and Cultural Transformations in early-modern Europe.* 2 Vols. Cambridge: Cambridge University Press.

Fish, Stanley
1980   *Is There a Text in This Class? The Authority of Interpretive Communities.* Cambridge, MA: Harvard University Press.

Fortna, Robert T.
1970   *The Gospel of Signs. A Reconstruction of the Narrative Source Underlying the Fourth Gospel. SNTS MS* 11. Cambridge: Cambridge University Press.

Frei, Hans W.
1974   *The Eclipse of Biblical Narrative. A Study in Eighteenth and Nineteenth Century Hermeneutics*. New Haven and London: Yale University Press.

Freud, Sigmund
1900   *Die Traumdeutung*. Leipzig and Vienna: Franz Deuticke [Eng. trans., *The Interpretation of Dreams*. New York: John Wiley & Sons, 1961].
1939   *Moses and Monotheism*. New York: Vintage Books.

Gadamar, Hans-Georg
1960   *Wahrheit und Methode. Grundzüge einer philosophischen Hermeneutik*. Tübingen: Mohr.

Gerhardsson, Birger
1961   *Memory and Manuscript. Oral Tradition and Written Transmission in Rabbinic Judaism and Early Christiantiy. ASNU 22.* Lund: C. W. K. Gleerup/Copenhagen: Ejnar Munksgaard.

Hägg, Thomas
1983   *The Novel in Antiquity*. Berkeley, CA: University of California Press.

Handelman, Susan A.
1982   *The Slayers of Moses. The Emergence of Rabbinic Interpretation in Modern Literary Theory*. Albany, N.Y.: State University of New York Press.

Havelock, Eric A.
1978   *The Greek Concept of Justice. From Its Shadow in Homer to Its Substance in Plato*. Cambridge, MA: Harvard University Press.

Hengel, Martin
1977   *Crucifixion in the ancient World and the Folly of the Message of the Cross*. Philadelphia, PA: Fortress Press.

Hoy, David Couzens
1978   *The Critical Circle. Literature and History in Contemporary Hermeneutics*. Berkeley, CA: University of California Press.

Iser, Wolfgang
1974   *The Implied Reader. Patterns of Communication in Prose Fiction from Bunyan to Beckett*. Baltimore, MD: Johns Hopkins University Press.
1978   *The Act of Reading. A Theory of Aesthetic Response*. Baltimore, MD: Johns Hopkins University Press.

Jauss, Hans Robert
1982   *Towards an Aesthetic of Reception*. Minneapolis, MN: University of Minnesota Press.

Kelber, Werner H.
1983   *The Oral and the Written Gospel. The Hermeneutics of Speaking*

and Writing in the Synoptic Tradition, Mark, Paul, and Q. Philadelphia, PA: Fortress Press.

1985   "From Aphorism to Sayings Gospel, and from Parable to Narrative Gospel." *FFF* (= *Facets and Foundation Forum)* 1: 1–8.

Kermode, Frank
1979   *The Genesis of Secrecy. On the Interpretation of Narrative.* Cambridge, MA and London: Harvard University Press.
1983   *The Art of Telling. Essays on Fiction.* Cambridge, MA: Harvard University Press.

Koester, Helmut
1983   "History and Development of Mark's Gospel (From Mark to Secret Mark and 'Canonical' Mark)." Pp. 35–57 in *Colloquy on New Testament Studies. A Time for Reappraisal and Fresh Approaches.* Macon, GA: Mercer University Press.

Krieger, Murray
1964   *A Window to Criticism. Shakespeare's Sonnets and Modern Poetics.* Princeton, N.J.: Princeton University Press.

Link, Hannelore
1976   *Rezeptionsforschung. Eine Einführung in Methoden und Probleme.* Stuttgart: Kohlhammer.

Ong, Walter J., S.J.
1967   *The Presence of the Word. Some Prolegomena for Cultural and Religious History.* New Haven, CT and London: Yale University Press. Paperback ed., Minneapolis, MN: University of Minnesota Press, 1981.
1977   *Interfaces of the Word. Studies in the Evolution of Consciousness and Culture.* Ithaca, N.Y. and London: Cornell University Press.
1982   Orality and Literacy. The Technologizing of the Word. London and New York: Methuen.

Pagels, Elaine
1981   "The Orthodox Against the Gnostics: Confrontation and Interiority in Early Christianity." In *The Other Side of God. A Polarity in World Religion.* Ed. Peter L. Berger. Garden City, N.Y.: Anchor Press, Doubleday.

Perkins, Pheme
1980   *The Gnostic Dialogue. The Early Church and the Crisis of Gnosticism.* New York: Paulist Press.

Peterson, Norman R.
1978   *Literary Criticism for New Testament Critics.* Philadelphia, PA: Fortress Press.

Polzin, Robert
1980   *Moses and the Deuteronomist. A Literary Study of the Deuteronomic History.* New York: Seabury Press.

Ricoeur, Paul
    1975   "Biblical Hermeneutics." *Semeia* 4: 27–148.
    1984   "From Proclamation to Narrative." *JR* 64: 501–12.

Robbins, Vernon K.
    1984   *Jesus the Teacher. A Socio-Rhetorical Interpretation of Mark*. Philadelphia, PA: Fortress Press.

Robinson, James M.
    1970   "On the Gattung of Mark (and John)." Pp. 99–129 in *Jesus and Man's Hope*, Vol. I, Pittsburgh, PA: Pittsburgh Theological Seminary.
    1982a   "On the Gattung of Mark (and John)." Pp. 11–39 in *The Problem of History in Mark and other Marcan Studies*. Philadelphia, PA: Fortress Press.
    1982b   "Gnosticism and the New Testament." Pp. 40–53 in *The Problem of History in Mark and other Marcan Studies*. Philadelphia, PA: Fortress Press
    1982c   "Jesus: From Easter to Valentinus (or to the Apostles' Creed)." *JBL* 101: 5–37
    1986   "The Gospels as Narative." Pp. 97–112 in *The Bible and the Narrative Tradition*. Ed. Frank McConnell. New York/Oxford: Oxford University Press.

Robinson, James M., and
Helmut Koester
    1971   *Trajectories through Early Christianity*. Philadelphia: Fortress Press.

Schneidau, Herbert N.
    1976   *Sacred Discontent. The Bible and Western Tradition*. Baton Rouge, LA: Louisiana State University Press.
    1978   "For Interpretation." *MoRev* 1: 70–88.
    1982   "The Word against the Word: Derrida on Textuality." *Semeia* 23: 5–28.
    1985   "Literary Relations Among the Gospels: Harmony or Conflict?" *Studies in the Literary Imagination* 18: 17–32.
    1986   "Biblical Narrative and Modern Consciousness." Pp. 132–50 in *The Bible and the Narrative Tradition*. Ed. Frank McConnell. New York/Oxford: Oxford University Press.

Scholes, Robert and
Robert Kellog
    1966   *The Nature of Narrative*. New York and London: Oxford University Press.

Morton Smith
    1973a   *The Secret Gospel. The Discovery and Interpretation of the Secret Gospel According to Mark*. New York: Harper & Row.

1973b   *Clement of Alexandria and a Secret Gospel of Mark*. Cambridge, MA: Harvard University Press.

1982   "Clement of Alexandria and Secret Mark: The Score at the End of the First Decade." *HTR* 75: 449–61.

Snell, Bruno
1960   *The Discovery of the Mind. The Greek Origins of European Thought*. New York: Harper & Row.

Stock, Brian
1983   *The Implications of Literacy. Written Language and Models of Interpretation in the Eleventh and Twelfth Centuries*. Princeton, N.J.: Princeton University Press.

Talbert, Charles H.
1977   *What is a Gospel? The Genre of the Canonical Gospels*. Philadelphia, PA: Fortress Press.

Tyler, Stephen A.
1978   *The Said and the Unsaid. Mind, Meaning, and Culture*. New York: Academic Press.

Via, Dan O.
1967   *The Parables. Their Literary and Existential Dimension*. Philadelphia: Fortress Press.

1975   *Kerygma and Comedy in the New Testament. A Structuralist Approach to Hermeneutic*. Philadelphia, PA: Fortress Press.

Vielhauer, Philipp
1975   *Geschichte der urchristlichen Literatur*. Berlin and New York: Walter de Gruyter.

Votaw, Clyde Weber
1970   *The Gospels and Contemporary Biographies in the Greco-Roman World*. Philadelphia: Fortress Press.

White, Hayden
1973   *Metahistory. The Historical Imagination in Nineteenth-Century Europe*. Baltimore, MD and London: Johns Hopkins University Press.

1978   *Tropics of Discourse. Essays in Cultural Criticism*. Baltimore, MD and London: Johns Hopkins University Press.

1980   "The Value of Narrativity in the Representation of Reality." *Critical Inquiry* 7: 5–27.

Wrede, William
1901   *Das Messiasgeheimnis in den Evangelien. Zugleich ein Beitrag zum Verständnis des Markusevangeliums*. Göttingen: Vandenhoeck & Ruprecht [Eng. trans., *The Messianic Secret*. Cambridge: T. and T. Clark, 1981].

Yates, Frances A.
1966   *The Art of Memory*. Chicago, IL: University of Chicago Press.

"LET THE READER UNDERSTAND"

Herbert N. Schneidau
University of Arizona

To an outsider like me, the work of Werner Kelber participates in what appears to be a paradigm-shift in New Testament studies. The lines of force in this transformation, as I apprehend them, are relatively clear: from the fragmentation of form-criticism and the search for pieces of the *ipsissima verba*, to a concern for narrative wholes, continuities, and resultant effects; from the assumption that gospel traditions flowed naturally or inevitably into their canonical receptacles, with the writers acting as mere recorders and redactors, to an apprehension of the writers' authorial and interpretive function, and of the individualistic and polemic character of their works; from a positivist assumption that the texts can be made to yield at least sequences of probabilities about the historical Jesus, to an interest in the portrayals as dramatizations in their own right, comparable in some respects to the history-plays of Shakespeare. Kelber's major contribution so far is to highlight the problems involved in the very shift of Christianity from a proclamation by itinerant preachers to a faith kept by communities and texts, a transition that presumably started no earlier than a generation and a half after Jesus' death. (Paul spoke to communities, but these were only beginning to develop their own traditions of interpretation and legend, the preconditions for textual production.)

Since neither interest in the earthly Jesus nor availability of circulating texts seems deducible from Paul's letters, the hypothesis that the gospels were mere by-products of the onflow of tradition is highly dubious. Kelber posits a fateful conflict between the oral dynamics of apostolic and prophetic preaching, with its predominant motif of embodied presence ("He who hears you hears me," as Jesus is made to say in Luke 10:16), and the historicizing implications of narrative texts, which among other things warn against "false Christs" who will say "I am he!" and "deceive many" (Mark 13:6, 22). It seems to me very likely that Mark is here warning against overzealous prophets who proclaim themselves to be voices or even reincarnations of the Christ, but even if not, the first narrative gospel tells a story of absence and frustration, rather than presence and fulfillment. Somewhere in this period, apparently, occurred the textualizing of sayings-collections, which mediate or perhaps disguise the cross-purposive clash of textuality with orality.

Cogent arguments from James M. Robinson and others urge us to see the narrative gospels as pushing the center of interest back from the gnomic and Gnostic wisdom of the resurrected "living Jesus," with his luminous appearances and esoteric teachings, toward the career of the earthly Jesus. Retrojections of the luminous appearances into the Transfiguration and perhaps even the walking-on-water stories become even more interesting possibilities in this context, as does the domestication of the sayings into fullblown discourses, with biographical settings, by the junior Synoptics. Is this pushing-back part of an anti-Gnostic campaign? If so, can Gnosticism be correlated with sayings-collections, against narrative and the stress on physicality (as in Luke-Acts) that became orthodoxy? Perhaps Kelber overstresses the hostility between the two forms: after all, Mark might have derived the theme of the blindness of the disciples from their obtuseness in *Thomas*—which is sometimes presented "dramatically," i.e. as incipient narrative. But it is also possible that there is even more in this clash than Kelber sees.

My sketch is intended as neither authoritative nor comprehensive, only to situate my own reactions and comments. As Chaucer's Parson says, "I speke under correccioun," and expect much of it not only from Kelber but from his interlocutors. But whatever the specialists decide about the various issues involved, I claim the *Narrenfreiheit* of the zealous amateur to offer what might be called literary reflections, without prejudice to the question Kelber himself raises as to how much of a move from the historical to the literary we are talking about.

Intertextuality as he sees it implied in the most recent work of John Dominic Crossan must certainly be debated, but texts are regularly overdetermined; many causes, including other texts, may impinge on them. Certainly Chaucer, Dante, and Aquinas worked in scribal contexts, yet they subsumed diverse texts into their own. For Mark to be diffusing several threatening texts throughout his own is not unthinkable; the other Synoptics, perhaps even John, did much the same with his work. And he could still be carrying on a polemic against oral prophets at the same time! With Kelber's voice to remind us of the dangers of transferring the assumptions of a typographic culture back into the ancient scribal context, I would judge that we are not in much danger of retrogressing to formalism. One way of augmenting Kelber's work, in fact, would be to look back at the career of Father Walter Ong, a major source for the concept of oral dynamic, and to note his running debate with the New Criticism, from the tracing of the "decay of dialogue" in Ramus *et al.* to the questioning of "well-wrought-urn-ism" (as I call it) in such essays as "A Dialectic of Aural and Objective Correlatives" and "The Jinni in the Well Wrought Urn." For Ong, the danger of formalism is loss or effacement of the idea of the work as personal utterance, or as dialogue, and its replacement by the idea of the work as artifact, a replacement aided by the use in criticism of a host of structural and object-related terms. Ong's war against formalism (seen also in the works of his friends Marshall McLuhan and Hugh Kenner) is a significant background to the contemporary questions, what is a text? What is an author? And what are reading and writing? Very few give the old formalist answers; even an "unreconstructed New Critic" like Harry Berger, Jr., would give answers that might puzzle Cleanth Brooks.

Biblical scholars need helpful, synthesizing introductions to these current debates and to their intramural histories. Available surveys like Frank Lentricchia's *After the New Criticism* (or Terry Eagleton's) have their own *parti pris* positions to advance, and cannot be taken as either objective or magisterial. This is not the place to assemble bibliographies, but I will simply remark that the latest work is not necessarily the best for the relevant purposes. For instance it is better to start with Fredric Jameson's *Prison-House of Language* than with his more recent, and more driven, work, such as *The Political Unconscious*, just as it is better to read Northrop Frye's *Anatomy of Criticism* than *The Great Code*. And I favor Peter Brooks' reappropriation of Freud in *Reading for the Plot* over the technocratic machinery of narratology *per se*, though the latter seem newer. As the late Paul de Man remarked, "Barthes, Genette, Todorov, Greimas, and their disciples all simplify and regress from Jakobson."[1] They go back to the old quest for foolproof methodologies. J. Hillis Miller has called these the "canny" critics, as against the "uncanny" like de Man himself.

It may even be that the gospels need a phase of formalist analysis before they come under the scrutiny of more currently popular methods such as reader-response or "reception" theory, although the basic questions of the latter, as of feminist and Marxist theory, are always germane. To prescribe a formalist phase may seem to presuppose an ontogeny-repeats-phylogeny authorization, but what I really have in mind is that today's positions are neither innocent nor historyless. There is no real harm to be done by experimenting with trendy methods, but indiscriminate enthusiasm for *le dernier cri* may efface the ground against which these figures have their signifying outlines—the Mona Lisa wouldn't look the same without the rocks. Indeed, the current modes of literary-theoretical discourse tend to cover up or brush away the traces of their own backgrounds. Whereas the work of Biblical scholars usually proceeds by a pre-Kuhnian accretive method, with careful citation of earlier workers and their propositions, literary theorists write as if they were making all things new. They seem to claim their own unique paradigms, and to emphasize discontinuity with predecessors: if these are brought in, it is for purposes of disagreement (and frequently mockery). Stanley Fish's recent texts are not exactly littered with footnotes. Such originalism has been especially plausible since the advent of deconstruction, which argues that a powerful determinism ("logocentrism" and its sub-stantialist congeners) has deformed our terminology: hence hyperbolical attempts to disown past discourses are warranted, because the danger of sliding back into "pre-owned" forms of thought is real.

But the result is that many theorists now write as if on the premises of Romantic "genius theory," which, by the mechanisms of the Freudian "family romance," gave us the transcendentalized notion of the author in the first place. In place of contingent human beings we got Godlike creators. In the nineteenth century, an author-folk synecdoche prevailed: that is, an author's greatness was ascribed to his embodiment in his work of the "genius" of his people, e.g. the "bardolatry" of Shakespeare. This evolved into assumptions that authors were geniuses in the vulgar sense, and thus the total masters and arbiters of their own works, even if unconscious creativity was theoretically allowed for; thus the meaning of a work like *Hamlet* is what Shakespeare *intended* by it. But struc-turalism, more persuasively than Marxism or Freudianism, has taught us that there are many codes of discourse implicated in a given work over which the author cannot conceivably have control or even awareness: at the very simplest level, in any randomized English message of sufficient length the letter "e" will appear most frequently. Any use of language is shaped by many forces, constraints, and precedents. Until recently, the modern reading of *Hamlet* was that it was about Hamlet's emotional problems; another age might have seen it as about the rights and rites of kingship. Who knows what Shakespeare intended? As Northrop Frye observed, if we could bring him back to question him as to the meaning of a particular speech, he would only say that he meant it to form part of the play—for that matter, any other reply would be as subject to interpre-tation as the original speech.

There is much more to say about the problem of authors' intentions, to be sure, but an amusing side issue surfaces here. Nothing so infuriates traditionalists such as Walter Jackson Bate and René Wellek, in their assaults on what they see as the new barbarism in literary studies, as the suspicion that critics today are putting themselves on a par with so-called creative writers. To the old guard, the schools of Fish and his rivals are not only meretricious, self-destructive, and so on, but also hubristically presumptuous. Such enthronement of authors is of course the last vestige of genius theory, and—more important—misses the point on which Kelber agrees with practically all current theorists, that narrative is a form of interpretation and vice versa. We have been taught to read philosophy as rhetoric by Derrida and others, historiography as narrative by Hayden White and others, and with the factitious nature of such discourse out in the open, we find the boundaries of genres to be highly problematic. To read the most objective statements and descriptions as literary tropes can be extremely illuminating: Edward Said reads Freud as a novel. My point is that we need no more of the leftover Romanticizing that has made the word "creative" into an American mystification. Just as *midrash* is obviously interpretation in the guise of added narrative, so even the most complacent positivist is verily writing fiction. This should indeed be implicit in the historical approach: we don't take Aristotle's statements at face value, but instead treat them as conditioned by the imaginative structures of his times.

Margaret Drabble, the English novelist and literary companion, writes of English landscape art: "The desire to turn landscape into art seems a natural one, though it is hard to say precisely why painters and writers should labour to reproduce in paint or words what each of us can see with our own eyes."[2] If representation were merely reproduction, there would be a problem, but as it is in fact interpretation, the difficulty disappears. Even a photograph is not a mere copy in this or Plato's sense, but has its own claims to advance, often about the nature of images. *A fortiori* for writing, in which the "referent" is simply an occasion. Writing never intends to efface itself in favor of its subject or model. As E. H. Gombrich observes in *Meditations on a Hobbyhorse*, the child's toy is neither imitative nor expressive (of its creator's personality, emotions, or the like). It is rather a representation that asserts something about the functional character of a horse, for certain purposes and in a certain light—here, the child's need to ride. The toy becomes in effect a horse in its own right, rather than a portrayal of a particular horse or a generalization about "horse-ness." So writing creates an intellectual experience not wholly subsumed into the supposed original, even if occasioned by and interpretive of it. The best analogy for the gospels, by this reasoning, is neither mirror nor transparent window, but perhaps stained-glass window. Through its representation we do not discern the original events (though we may see a vista from which certain deductions can be drawn about the uses to which the object has been put); rather, if we want to find out about the contexts of the creation, we must pay attention to the details of the workmanship.

Any author of narrative, whether of outright fiction or history or historicized fiction such as much of the Bible, is an illusionist. And so great is the force of his mode of discourse that it is very hard to stop participating in his events vicariously, so as to look for the wizard behind the machinery. Lacking a Toto to run behind the curtain, we must keep asking ourselves: where is he selecting, controlling? Why does he leave out *this* and include *that?* And where are other forces controlling him, creating their own necessities? One way to focus is to stop after every sentence, cover the rest, and imagine the range of sentences that may follow. Some junctures are better for this purpose than others, obviously, but we need such artificial devices to keep from falling back into complicity: we have an overpowering tendency to make a "video" of the events. Even though mostly written in the past tense, narratives have an astonishing presentness, as if the scene were unrolling before us. Indeed, the most amazing thing about narrative is not its ubiquity in human cultures, but its power. All but the clumsiest and most obviously contrived tales will make us imaginative participants. I have argued elsewhere that this cannot simply be taken as a given, but must have to do with the nature of man as a verbal animal, and with the possibility that consciousness itself is at least latently a narrative mode; so that I disagree somewhat with Hayden White, quoted by Kelber: we do live in story, in fact nowhere else, and we are always seeing ourselves as the main figures in the story of our lives, as we imagine scenarios for whatever swims into our ken. Consciousness is in fact a fantasy, keyed to certain sensory processes; and as dreams and hallucinations show, the control is inside us: Coleridge knew that perception is a creative act. Our Western consciousness seems particularly introspective and individualistic, which may be due to the Bible—not only the narratives, but also the prophets' exhortations, for these too are imaginative writings.

To entertain this possibility is to raise afresh the old question about the uniqueness of the Judeo-Christian tradition. Somewhat unfashionably, I hold that the Bible does possess a distinctive character that contains some of the keys to our relatively restless and changeful cultural traditions. Unless our volatility were merely a by-product of industrialism, I see no better explanation, and industrialism itself is hardly an accident, much less a "progress." In terms of narrative: the "story," from tribal times (if we may judge by, say, Lévi-Strauss' Bororo) to Aristotle, has as its function the manifestation of the *logos*, the cosmic constitution or blueprint, the rationale for the way things are and always must be. Whether an episodic necklace on which the *bricoleur* strings mythemes, or as *mimesis* of causal explanation, it tells of the necessary structure and nature of things. For Aristotle tragedy is as such superior to history, since actual events present only a very limited view of the *logos*, compared to a poetic condensation and idealization of them—what actually happened is less important than what might or should have happened. The gospel story is of an irruption, not of the way things always are; it is not typical or illustrative, as even the Oedipus story is (John's *logos* is, as we say, another story). For this among other reasons, it is not within the classical purview.

The Bible reverses Aristotle's preferences, and relies on history instead of philosophy (or tragedy). As James Barr notes, we tend to underestimate the point that the Bible consists largely of ("history-like") narratives rather than doctrinal statements. But what does history mean in the Bible? Surely not the positivist notion of a record of events; as to that, are not those things written in the Book of the Chronicles of the Kings of Israel and Judah? History is rather the proclamation of God's unpredictable acts (for me, the *Geschichte/Historie* distinction is not outdated). But the main point is that it is a theme as well as a mode, one that emphasizes reversals of expectation, unlikely choices (sometimes laughable ones), the emergence of the obscure and the uplifting of the downtrodden, with all manner of paradoxical overturning and of apparently arbitrary intervention. Why does God prefer Abel's sacrifice, save Noah, select Abram, miraculously grant Isaac and then demand his sacrifice? Such reasons as are given are lamely after-the-fact; because his acts seem arbitrary, we know they are divine, beyond us (Rom. 9:6–33). As Harold Bloom says, J's Yahweh is one of the great uncanny figures, worthy of Kafka. In its hortatory aspect, history is even more the opposite of the *logos:* whereas the rule from tribal cultures to the Greeks was that social order is valorized because it recapitulates cosmic order (see Lévi-Strauss on the Oedipus myth), Biblical history urges freedom from the constraints of even the mightiest or most seductive cultures, as all the *exodoi* attest: Noah out of his world, Abram out of Ur, Lot out of Sodom, Moses and Israel out of Egypt—stories like these combine with Joshua vs. Jericho and the kings, Gideon vs. Midian, Samson and Saul and David vs. the Philistines, and a host of others, on down to Daniel's visions of the fall of empires. The theme of the underdog may have become hackneyed today, but what evidence is there that it was even known before the Bible? History in the Bible is innovatively anti-imperialist, (often) anti-monarchical, always questioning or calling to account the very existence of culture, one's own (Amos *et al.*) as well as those of powerful overlords. Where do we find this anticipated in the ancient world? Lévi-Strauss has shown that in normative cultures the main intellectual effort has to be devoted to a kind of thought which, whether as myth or taxonomy, ultimately is as logocentric as Aristotle's: it shows how things fit into systems, how they are and must be, culturally and naturally.

Biblical history is presented as what the Elizabethans would have called a "mirror for magistrates," a set of stories to remind us of our limitations and of the powers above us. It confounds the *logos* and the lessons the wise would derive from it. It disquiets the great, unsettles the self-satisfied, and solaces the poor. For me, the folly/wisdom contrast in 1 Corinthians, like that of the absurd/expectable in Tertullian's "credo quia absurdum," typifies Judeo-Christian "history." Whereas wisdom is always logocentric. (Perhaps this fits into the Gnostic/narrative contrast.) This view may be attacked as slighting to Judaism, as propagating the old law-gospel distinction, as a remnant of neo-orthodoxy, etc. But suppose that it corresponds to what Mark would have known as "history": would that not explain much about the paradoxical, parabolic quality of his narrative?

If my view is valid, it suggests much of the reason for the hypertro-

phy of individualism in the West as well as its volatility. In tribal cultures,
those stories and myths survived that used the *mimesis* of "the way things
happen" in the same way that poetry uses sound-structures, to provide
memorability for the needful themes, motifs, and lessons, as determined
by the culture's continuous need for self-replication; these are all implicitly collective. In Greek narratives the schoolboy was taught to see
himself as a solid citizen of the *polis*, ready to die for it, eager to imitate
Achilles not in his spiteful self-indulgence but rather in his willingness to
sacrifice long life for great glory (or, as Philip Slater suggests, to the
insane competitiveness for *aretē:* see *The Glory of Hera*). Oedipus
teaches you to accept your fate, and to become a blessing to your
community instead of a curse; Odysseus teaches you to get home in spite
of all obstacles, no matter what tricks and disguises you have to use.
(These readings resemble undergraduates' interpretations of *The Great
Gatsby* as a warning against too much partying.) But in the Bible
variations of the theme of exodus predominate, and the very word
"Hebrew" may mean something like *outlaw*. If a Greek hero leaves
home, it is to found a city; the Hebrew is likely to wander in the desert,
or even serve as a Philistine mercenary! In short the Bible seems to
proffer to its readers a more singular view of themselves (see Robert
Alter's contrast of the Priam-Achilles encounter with the death of David's
first son from Bathsheba, in *The Art of Biblical Narrative*). A text like
Mark seems to address inner resolve far more than group solidarity, in
spite of its probable communitarian context. This may be diluted slightly
in the other gospellers, but if so the disparity may be due to Mark's well-
known theme of withstanding persecution: a Christian could hardly face
death by calling on his innate loyalty to a clan or *polis*. He needed inner
resources, and an individualistic imperative: do NOT imitate the pillars
of the community, the self-styled insiders, those who wither in the sun.

Mark makes an excellent text to which to apply all the techniques I
mentioned, and those I didn't. Reading him makes me want to ask a
range of questions: what constitutes for him development, transition, and
the like? (Narratological.) How does he want what comes before to link
up with what comes after? (Formalist.) How does he establish his authority, and his relation to his reader? ("Reception.") On the last, note
how his abrupt proclamatory style (and unique use of *euaggelion*) contrasts with the others: Matthew arrogates to himself a scribe's authority
by displaying genealogy, Luke sophisticatedly offers to correct forerun-
ners, and John claims knowledge of the beginnings of all things. On the
other hand Mark sets a style for the others by being individualistic
through being universalistic. His implied readers are not Jews, certainly,
but his striking lack of other insular references indicates that he writes for
those who know something of the story but need authoritative interpretation. Above all, in his very famous apostrophe in Chapter 15—an apos-

trophe heard round the world, I would say—he appeals not to the one who reads the story out loud to others: what would be the point of his understanding if the others didn't? On the contrary, his implied reader is first of all an individual—even if Bultmann was right that it refers to "he who reads" Daniel (see TDNT s.v. *anaginoskō*).

But if the reader is going to understand, he must not rely solely on his unaided inner resources: there is an implicit appeal to those aspects of other interpretations that require revision. As Kelber says, the issue of revisionism is central: he quotes Gerald Bruns on Scripture's constant metamorphoses of itself, a point made by Erich Auerbach as well. If Auerbach and others who assert a bad fit between the gospels and antiquity's traditional genres are right, the dynamics of revision are far more important than the vexed question of the genre of the gospels: the significant literary ancestor of the gospels is not Plutarch, not the life of Apollonius, nor any aretalogy, but rather the Old Testament, the most revisionist of all texts. The early Christian habit of searching the prophets is manifest in the gospels, but originally the searchers may have been looking less for coded predictions of Jesus' birth and fate than at the startling challenges to Israel's comforting slogans and saws.

Kelber points out that if *Thomas* and other sayings-collections are gospels, then the question of genre has been misconceived in any case. It is worth noting that the gospels did not give rise to a long-lasting form, but remained *ad hoc*. And if the canonical gospels were "literary monstrosities" in their time, why not assume that Mark aimed at just this effect? He had no particular reason to offer readers a kind of text that would have a familiar shape; his urgencies seem rather to have moved him to lead the reader through a singular and intense experience, breathtaking in its implications. As Morton Enslin but not many other scholars emphasized, Mark is readable at a sitting, which makes it different from much ancient literature, including the other canonicals. Such considerations validate the new quest for narrative wholes. From proof-text to form-critical to structuralist analyses, atomization was the rule that prevented us from seeing these points, but now they seem salient. Atomization was appropriate to an age that sought to find the elementary building-blocks of matter, but physics has given up the substantialist conceptions that lay behind that search.

Some last thoughts: Kelber does well to warn us against conceiving of scribal texts as hermetically self-enclosed like a Mallarmé poem, but here we may need more literary reflections. The originality of New Criticism lay in its efforts to focus on the text rather than on the cumbrous and distracting masses of biography, philology, etc., that came to usurp the attention of traditional literary studies. C. S. Singleton, the great Dante scholar, once remarked that in his youth it was typical to study the sources of the *Decameron* in one semester, and its influences in the next,

never the text itself. With the New Critics there came about a paradigm
of self-referentiality, but although one may still hear versions of its axioms
from some semioticians, they have an old-fashioned ring. More distracting today are programmatic insistences, typically by Marxist critics, that
we must rehabilitate the "referent." Such calls belong to a disingenuous
campaign against the "aestheticism" of all other schools. Some, indeed,
seem to want to impose loyalty oaths for "social responsibility." The
danger here is a form of sentimentalism.

The notion of intertextuality has a similarly interesting ancestry in
Woölflin's famous observation that all paintings owe more to other paintings than they do to Nature. Texts are likely to be produced by reflection
on other texts rather than by reflection on the subject—though as I
suggested in Mark's case, perhaps with startling innovations. In Western
art as opposed to "conceptual" art (which is logocentric) the norm is not
slight variations on tightly fixed patterns: still, in literature, the contexts
for a text are other texts. Now, Derridaean assertions that there is nothing
outside the text are a little different: they refer to the irreducibly verbal
character of human existence, and to our anxiety to evade recognition of
this character by founding our language in "reality." This anxiety has
given us a vested interest in banishing texts and writing, making them
into *pharmakoi;* Derrida mischievously subverts the Platonic logic used
to justify this urge to expel the "secondary," the "parasitic." ("It's not we
who are unreal, it's merely writing, which is a copy at several removes,
etc.") But all language, it turns out, can be shown to have that alien
character for which writing was excoriated, and all experience (insofar as
it is experience and not mere sensation) has certain linguistic properties.
So our demotion of texts—habitual even in a text-centered age, when we
still ascribe sincerity and truth to "voice"—can be mocked by claiming
that all, in a sense, is text. Derrida's line of thought can lead to a subtle,
inveigling idea of intertextuality: we are the intersections of our quotations, the pieces of language we inherit and must work hard to identify.

I look forward eagerly to more correlations between literary criticism
and Biblical studies, but there are going to be more than a few cul-de-
sacs. Kelber points to dangers in uninformed acceptance of contemporary premises: I would dig for still more hidden agendas. For instance,
the greatest danger of the New Critical heritage, as I see it, is not
formalist hermeticism, but a deadly moralism that almost always crept
into its readings. Marvin Mudrick wonderfully parodies this: "*Macbeth*
teaches the important lesson that it's a mistake to be wrong." A depress-
ing number of twentieth-century readings have been afflicted by a need
for self-justification along the lines of liberal-humanist pieties, typically
producing premature if not empty ethical pronouncements. If sentimen-
tally adopted, these can be as great a danger as the dregs of apologetic
still disfiguring Biblical studies. But, luckily, the revisionist nature of our

culture nurtures a mutual and self-critical vigilance, our most valuable
habit.

NOTES

[1] Paul de Man, "Semiology and Rhetoric," reprinted in *Textual Strategies,* ed. Josue Harari
(Ithaca: Cornell University Press, 1979), 124.

[2] Margaret Drabble, *A Writer's Britain* (London: Thames and Hudson, 1979), 7.

www.ingramcontent.com/pod-product-compliance
Lightning Source LLC
Chambersburg PA
CBHW022135080426
42734CB00006B/366